GRIT

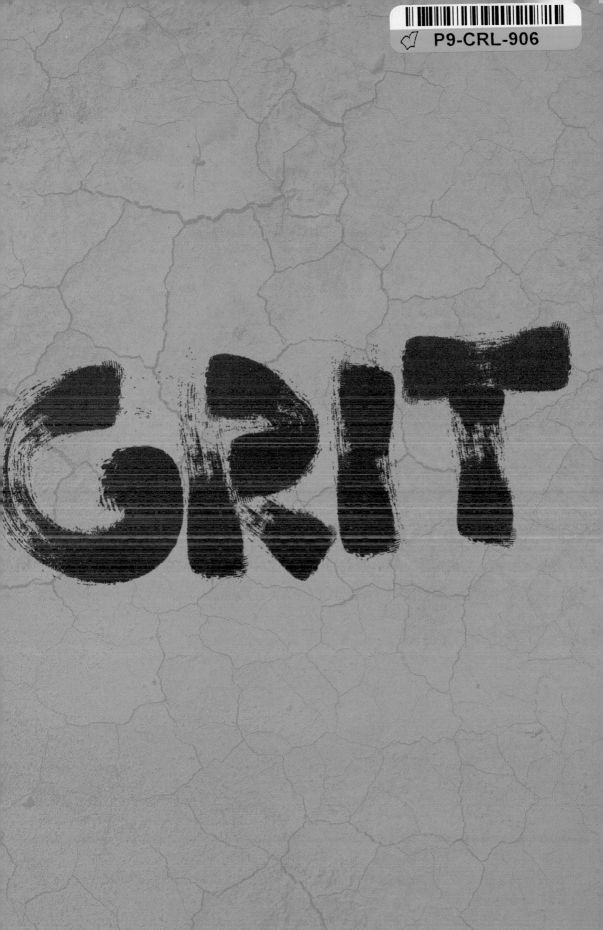

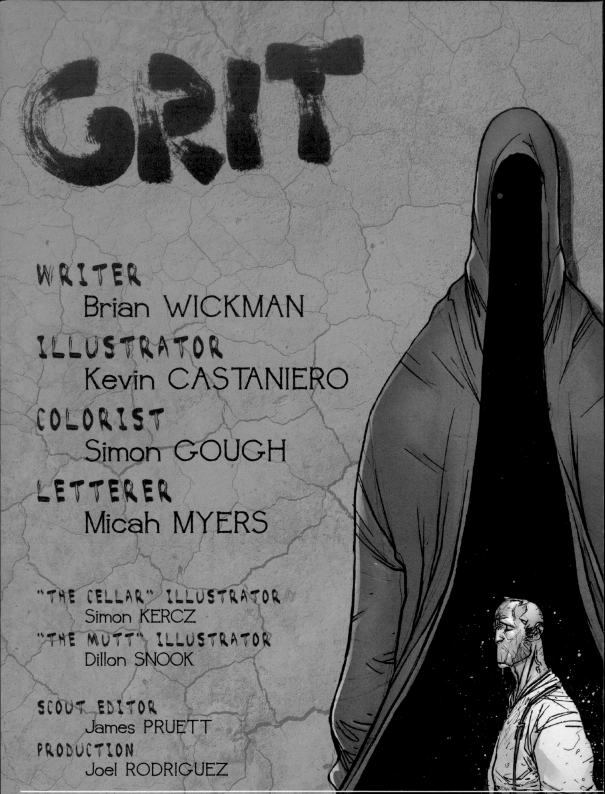

GRIT

WRITER
Brian WICKMAN

ILLUSTRATOR
Kevin CASTANIERO

COLORIST
Simon GOUGH

LETTERER
Micah MYERS

"THE CELLAR" ILLUSTRATOR
Simon KERCZ

"THE MUTT" ILLUSTRATOR
Dillon SNOOK

SCOUT EDITOR
James PRUETT

PRODUCTION
Joel RODRIGUEZ

SCOUT COMICS

Brendan Deneen, *CEO*
James Pruett, *CCO*
Tennessee Edwards, *CSO*
James Haick III, *President*

Don Handfield, *CMO*
David Byrne, *Co-Publisher*
Charlie Stickney, *Co-Publisher*
Joel Rodriguez, *Head of Design*

FB/TW/IG:
@Scoutcomics

LEARN MORE AT:
www.scoutcomics.com

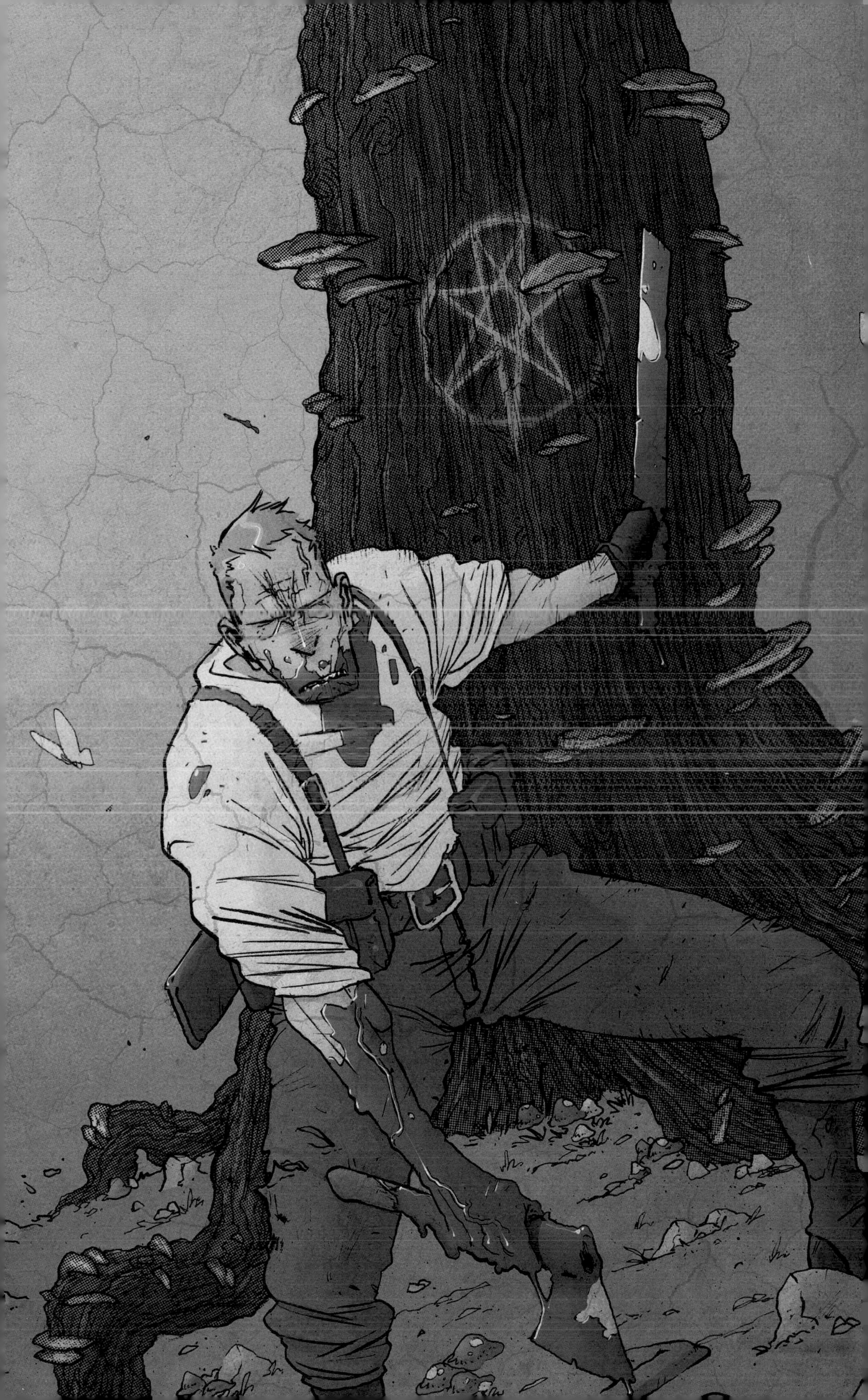

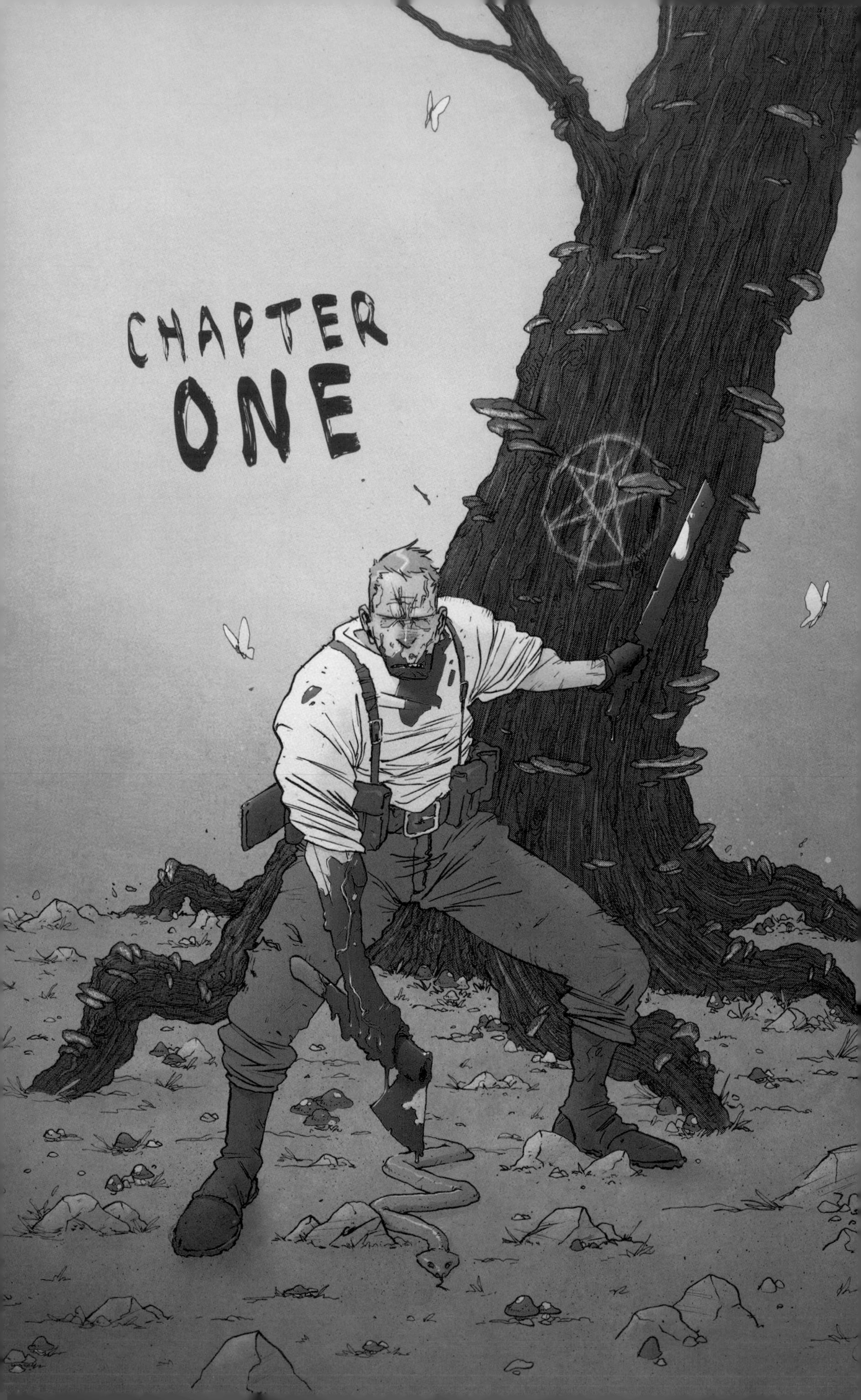
CHAPTER
ONE

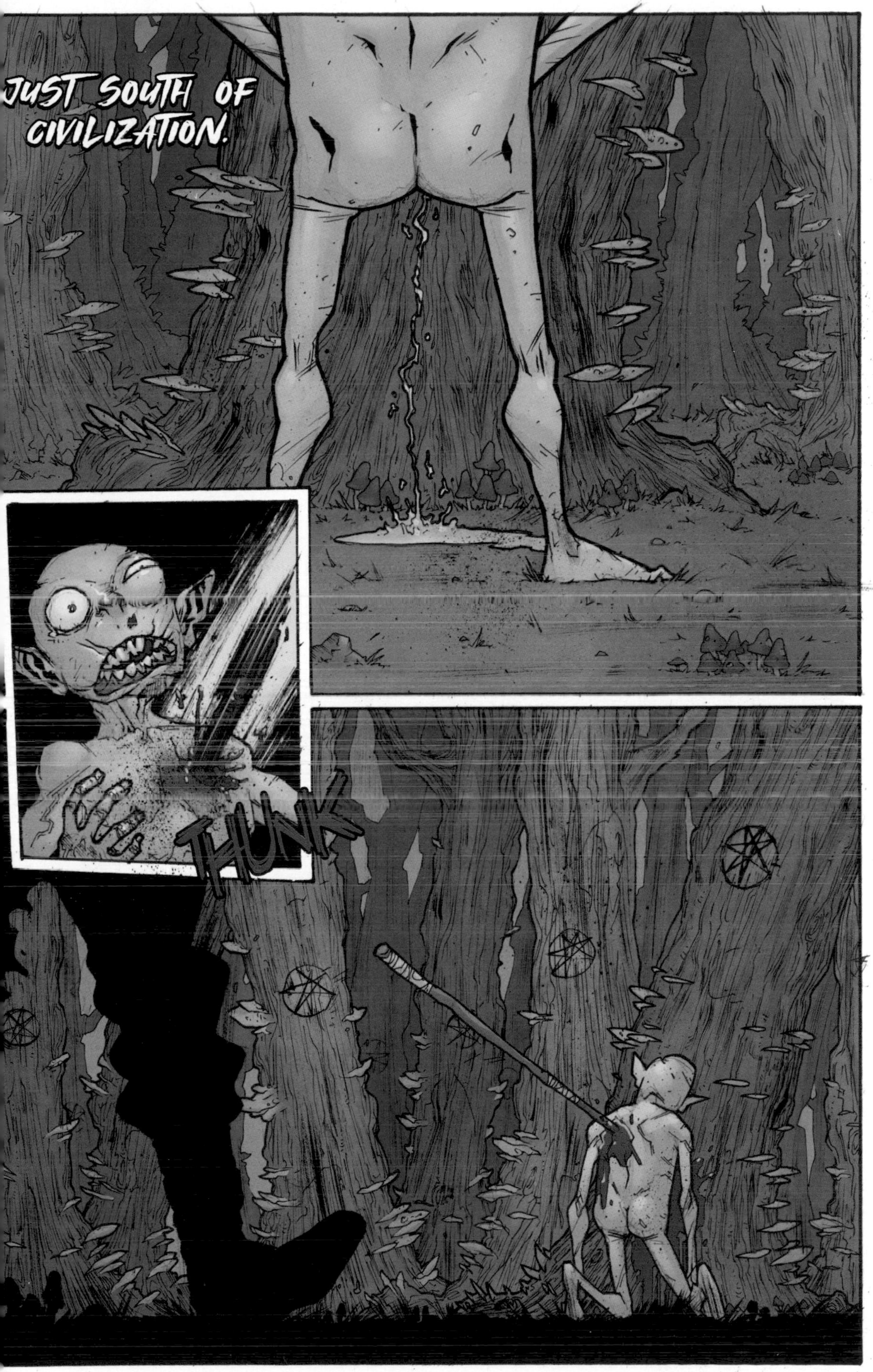
JUST SOUTH OF CIVILIZATION.
THUNK

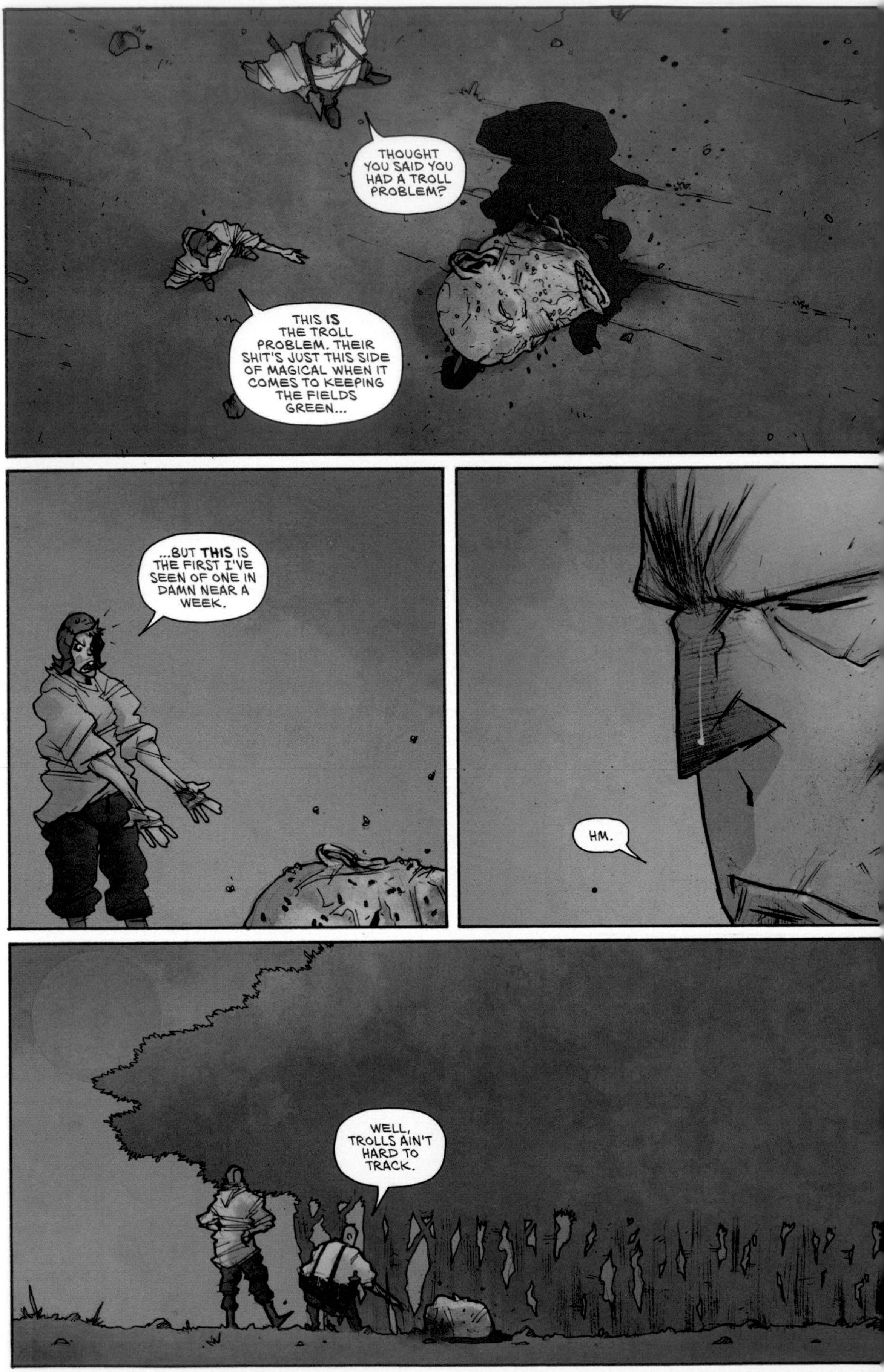
THOUGHT YOU SAID YOU HAD A TROLL PROBLEM?
THIS IS THE TROLL PROBLEM. THEIR SHIT'S JUST THIS SIDE OF MAGICAL WHEN IT COMES TO KEEPING THE FIELDS GREEN...
...BUT THIS IS THE FIRST I'VE SEEN OF ONE IN DAMN NEAR A WEEK.
HM.
WELL, TROLLS AIN'T HARD TO TRACK.

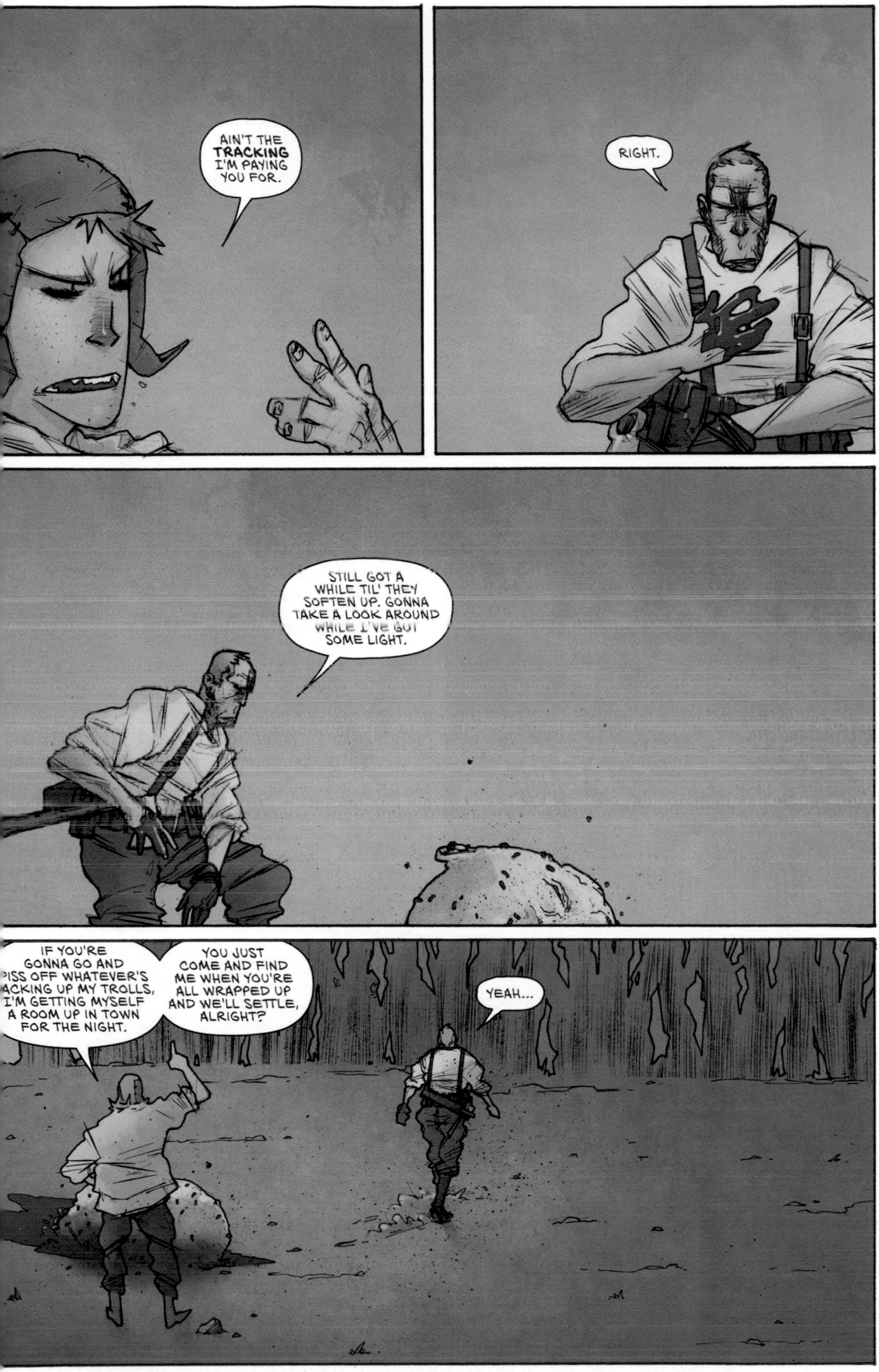
AIN'T THE **TRACKING** I'M PAYING YOU FOR.
RIGHT.
STILL GOT A WHILE TIL' THEY SOFTEN UP. GONNA TAKE A LOOK AROUND WHILE I'VE GOT SOME LIGHT.
IF YOU'RE GONNA GO AND PISS OFF WHATEVER'S ACKING UP MY TROLLS, I'M GETTING MYSELF A ROOM UP IN TOWN FOR THE NIGHT.
YOU JUST COME AND FIND ME WHEN YOU'RE ALL WRAPPED UP AND WE'LL SETTLE, ALRIGHT?
YEAH...

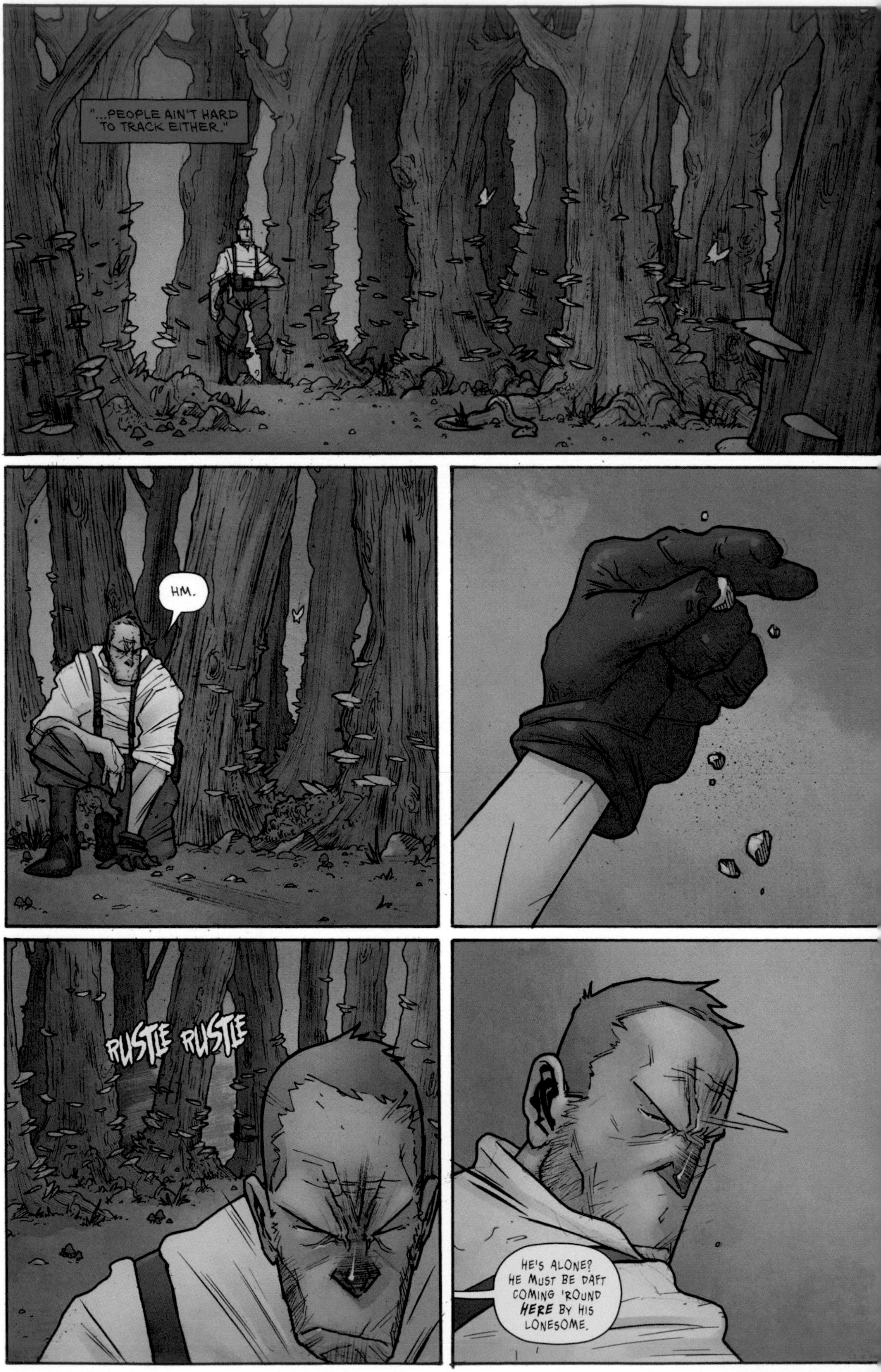
"...PEOPLE AIN'T HARD TO TRACK EITHER."
HM.
RUSTLE RUSTLE
HE'S ALONE? HE MUST BE DAFT COMING 'ROUND HERE BY HIS LONESOME.

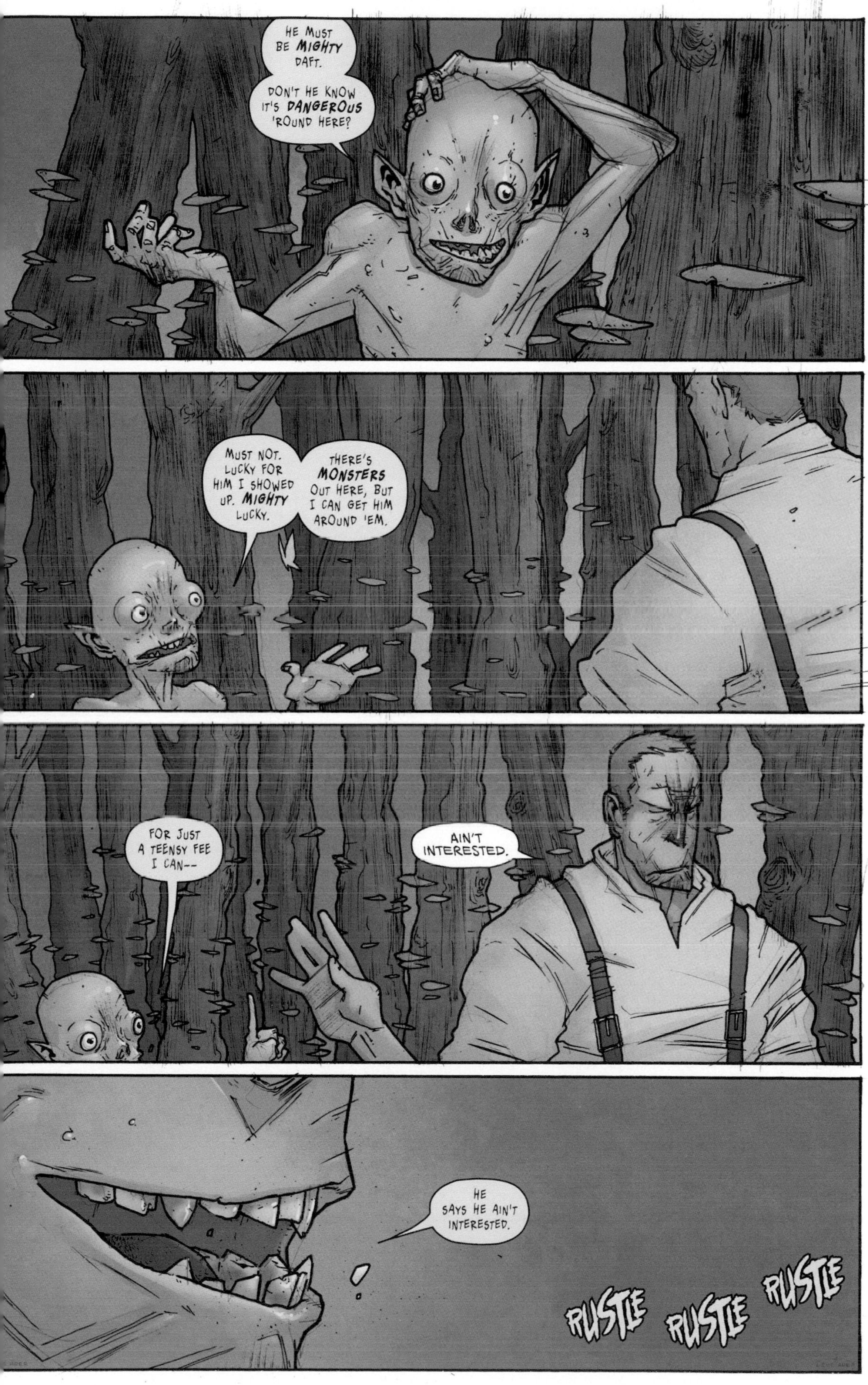
HE MUST BE MIGHTY DAFT.
DON'T HE KNOW IT'S DANGEROUS 'ROUND HERE?
MUST NOT. LUCKY FOR HIM I SHOWED UP. MIGHTY LUCKY.
THERE'S MONSTERS OUT HERE, BUT I CAN GET HIM AROUND 'EM.
FOR JUST A TEENSY FEE I CAN--
AIN'T INTERESTED.
HE SAYS HE AIN'T INTERESTED.
RUSTLE RUSTLE RUSTLE

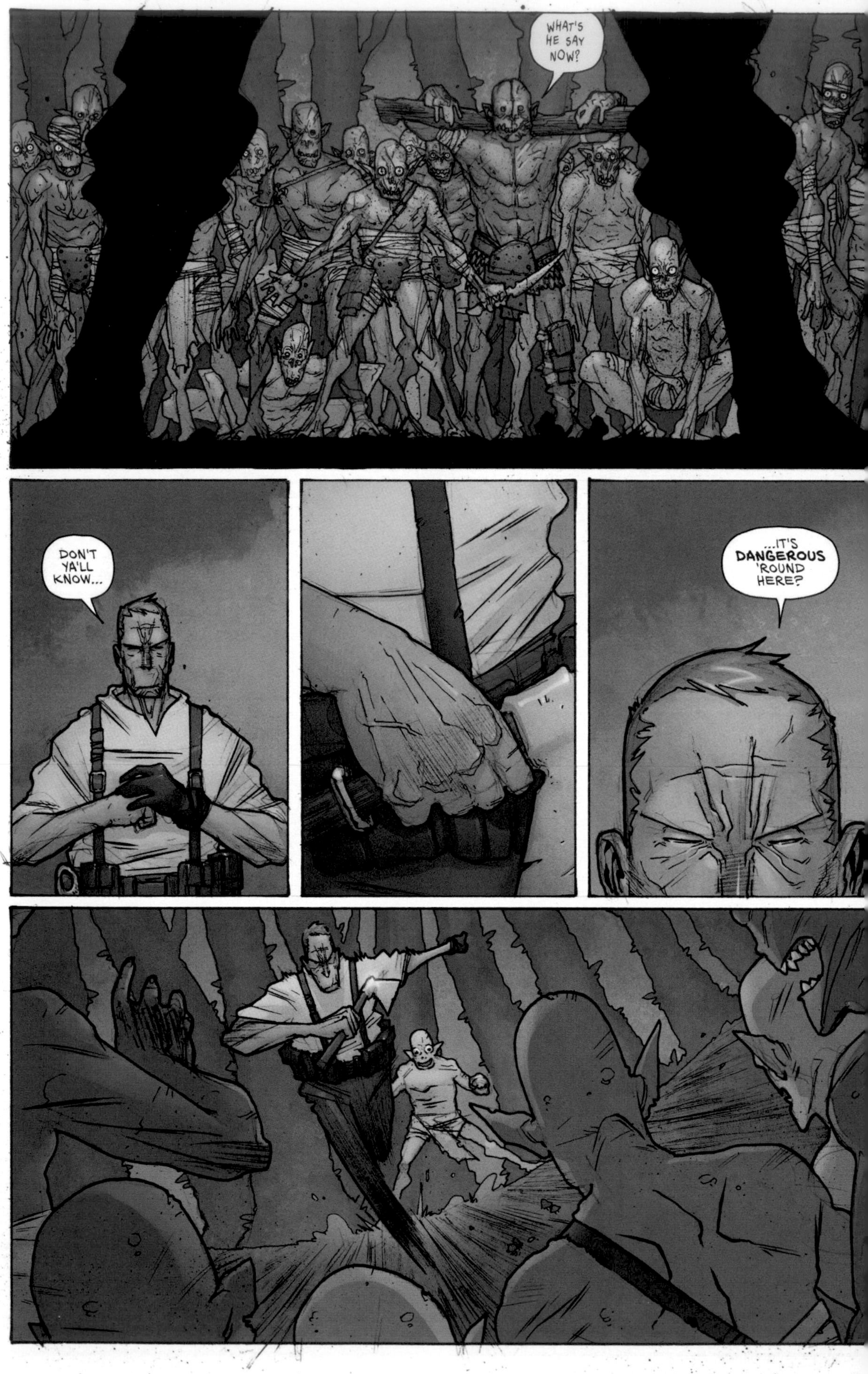
WHAT'S HE SAY NOW?
DON'T YA'LL KNOW...
...IT'S **DANGEROUS** 'ROUND HERE?

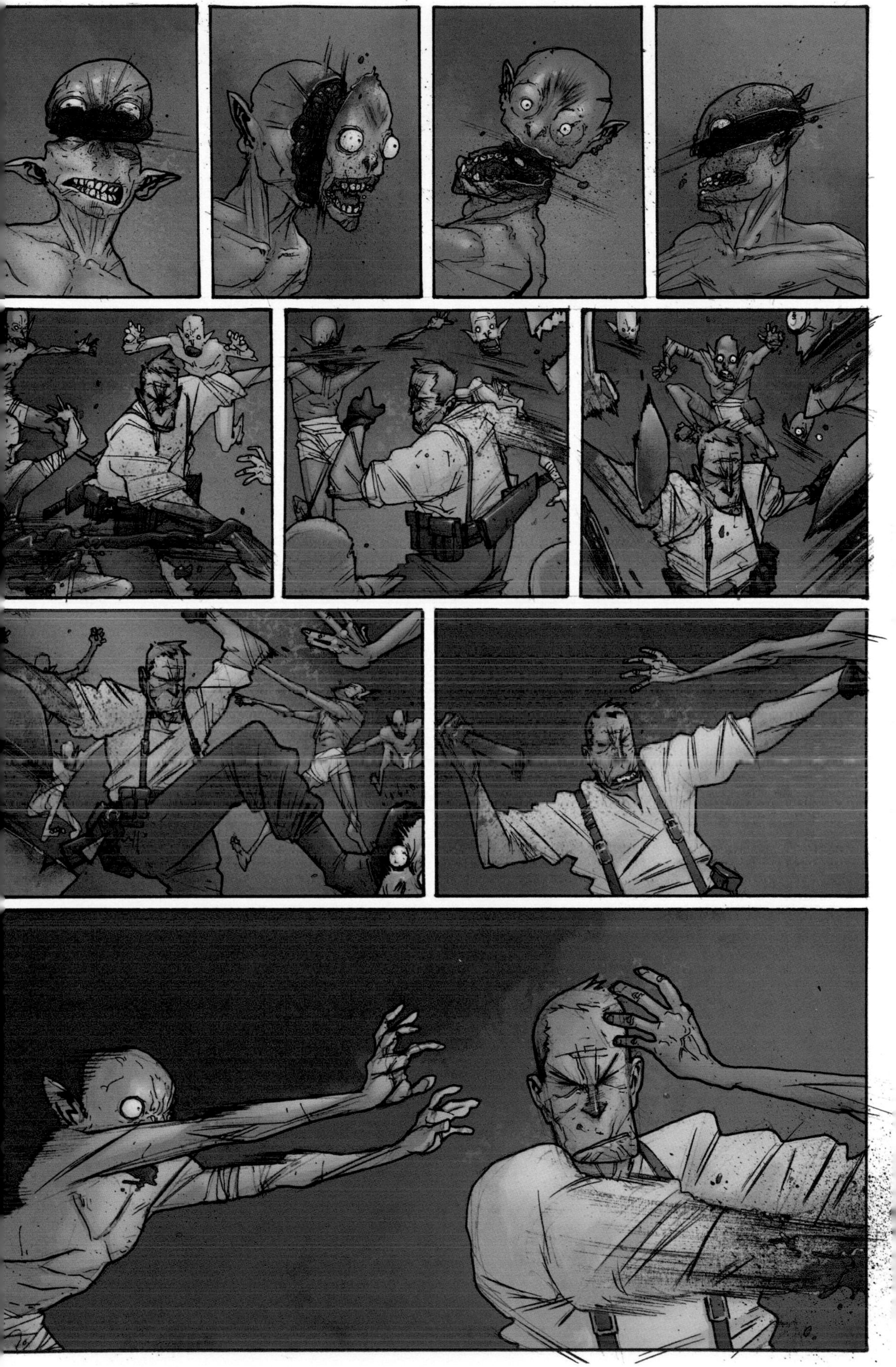

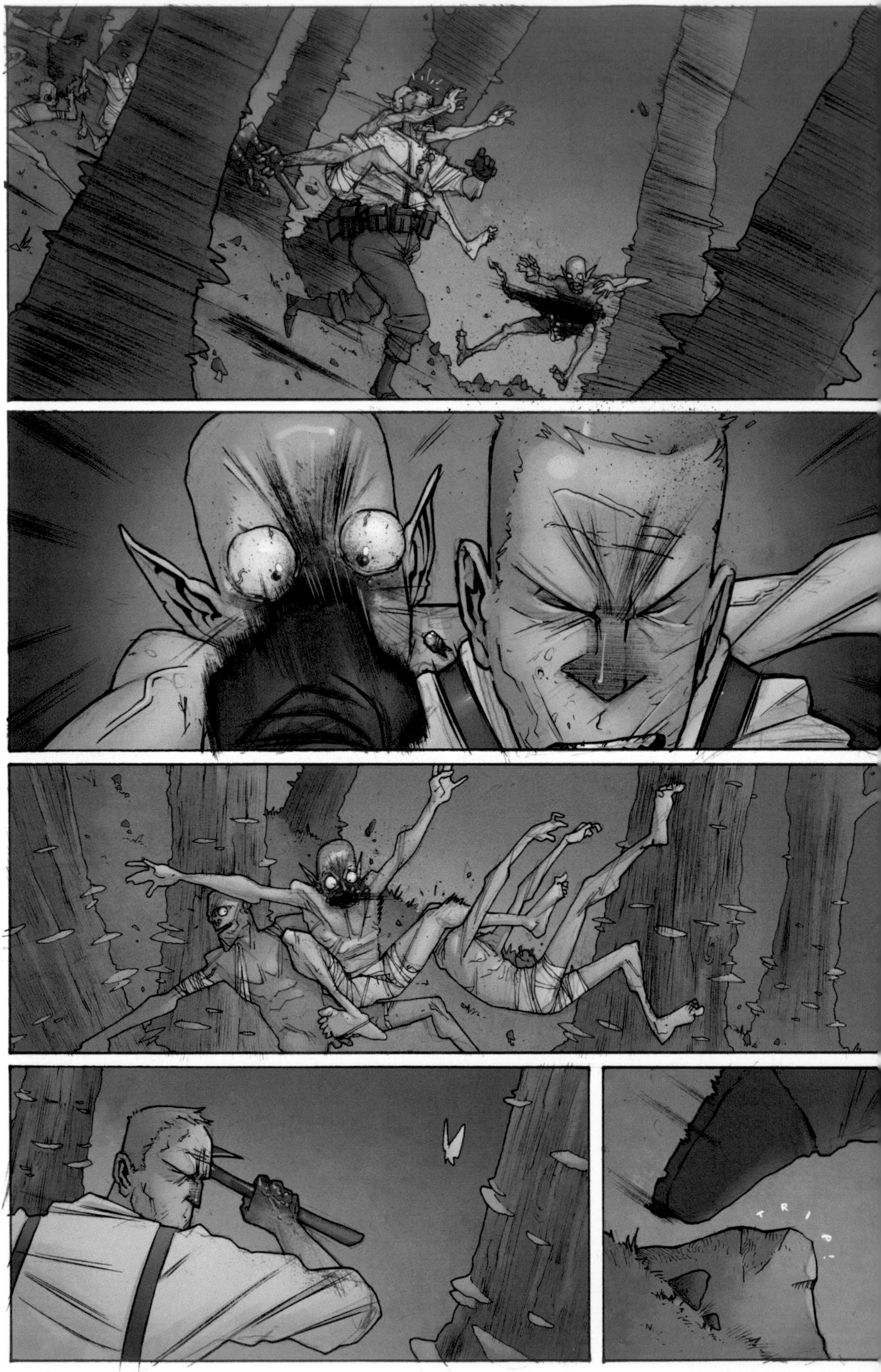
TRIP!

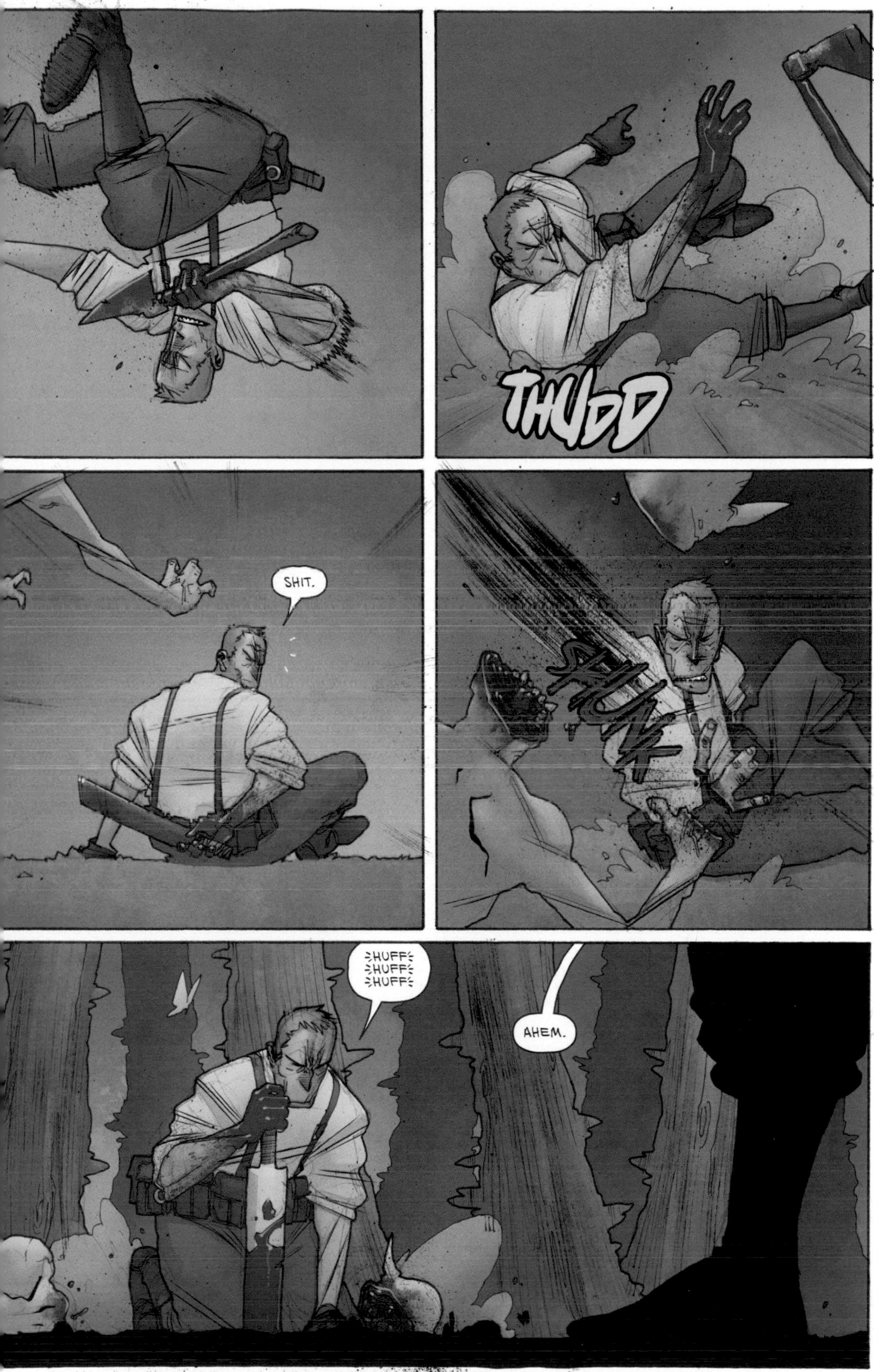
THUDD
SHIT.
SHUNK
HUFF HUFF HUFF
AHEM.

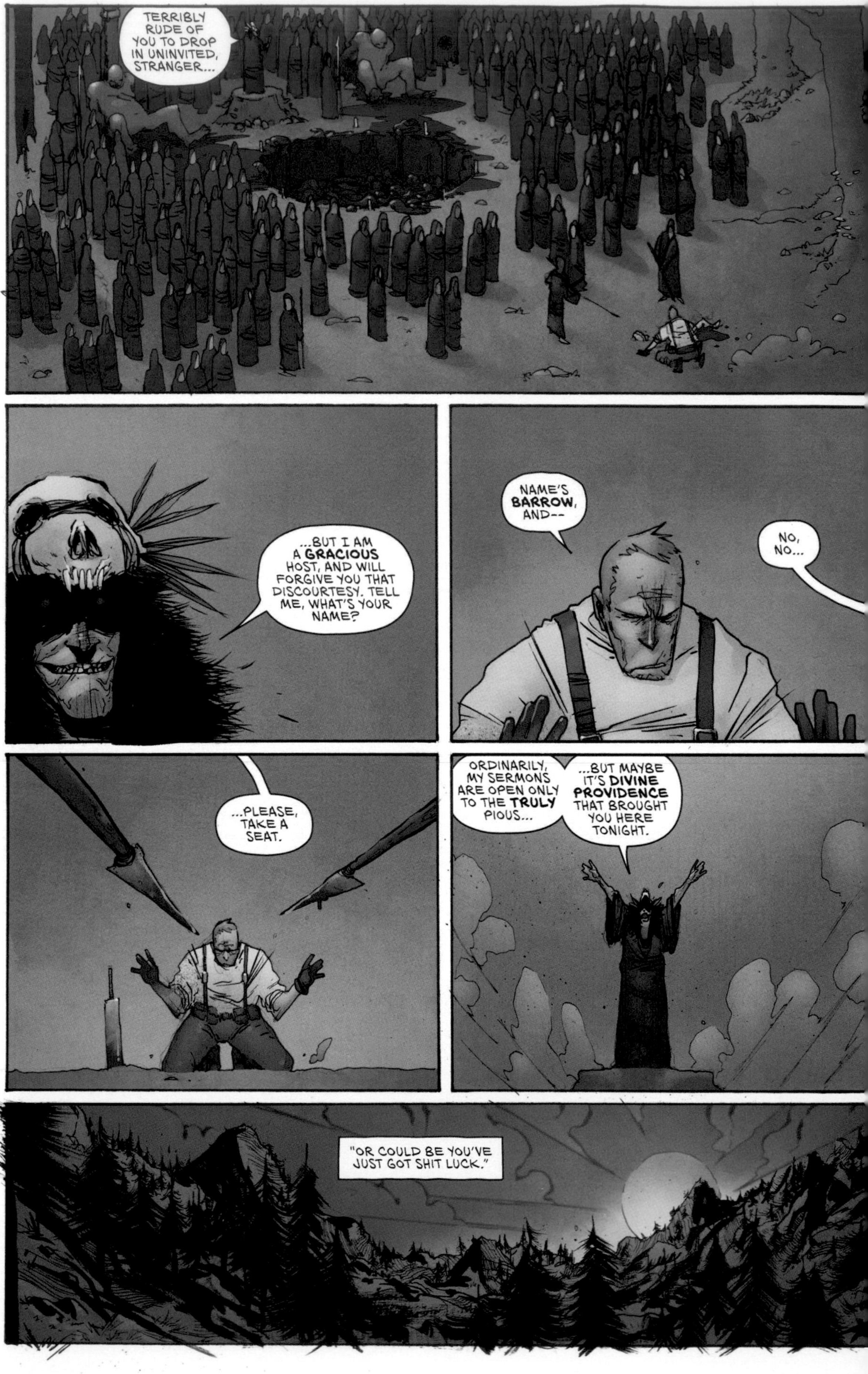
TERRIBLY RUDE OF YOU TO DROP IN UNINVITED, STRANGER...
...BUT I AM A GRACIOUS HOST, AND WILL FORGIVE YOU THAT DISCOURTESY. TELL ME, WHAT'S YOUR NAME?
NAME'S BARROW, AND--
NO, NO...
...PLEASE, TAKE A SEAT.
ORDINARILY, MY SERMONS ARE OPEN ONLY TO THE TRULY PIOUS...
...BUT MAYBE IT'S DIVINE PROVIDENCE THAT BROUGHT YOU HERE TONIGHT.
"OR COULD BE YOU'VE JUST GOT SHIT LUCK."

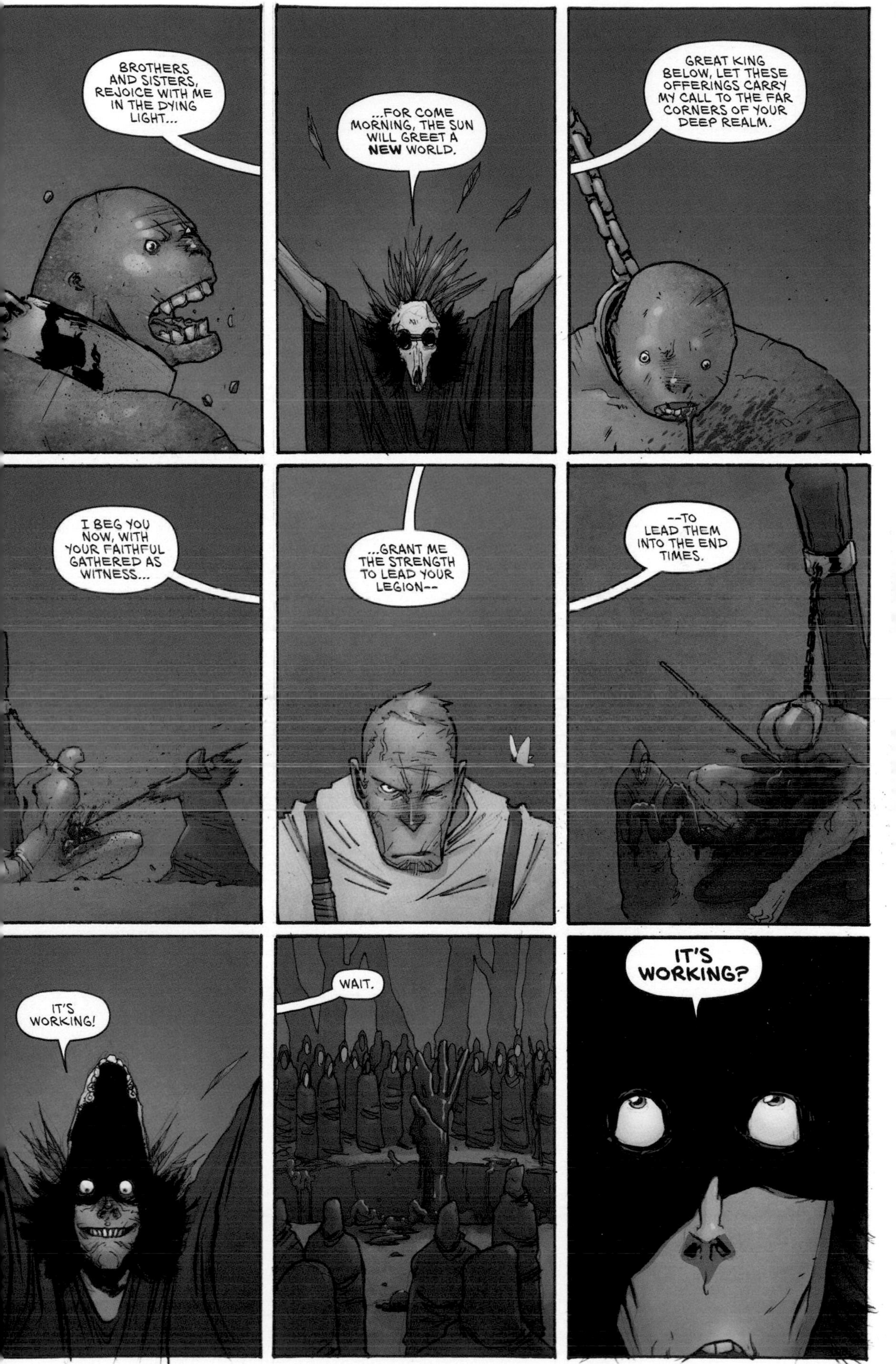
BROTHERS AND SISTERS, REJOICE WITH ME IN THE DYING LIGHT...
...FOR COME MORNING, THE SUN WILL GREET A **NEW** WORLD.
GREAT KING BELOW, LET THESE OFFERINGS CARRY MY CALL TO THE FAR CORNERS OF YOUR DEEP REALM.
I BEG YOU NOW, WITH YOUR FAITHFUL GATHERED AS WITNESS...
...GRANT ME THE STRENGTH TO LEAD YOUR LEGION--
--TO LEAD THEM INTO THE END TIMES.
IT'S WORKING!
WAIT.
IT'S WORKING?

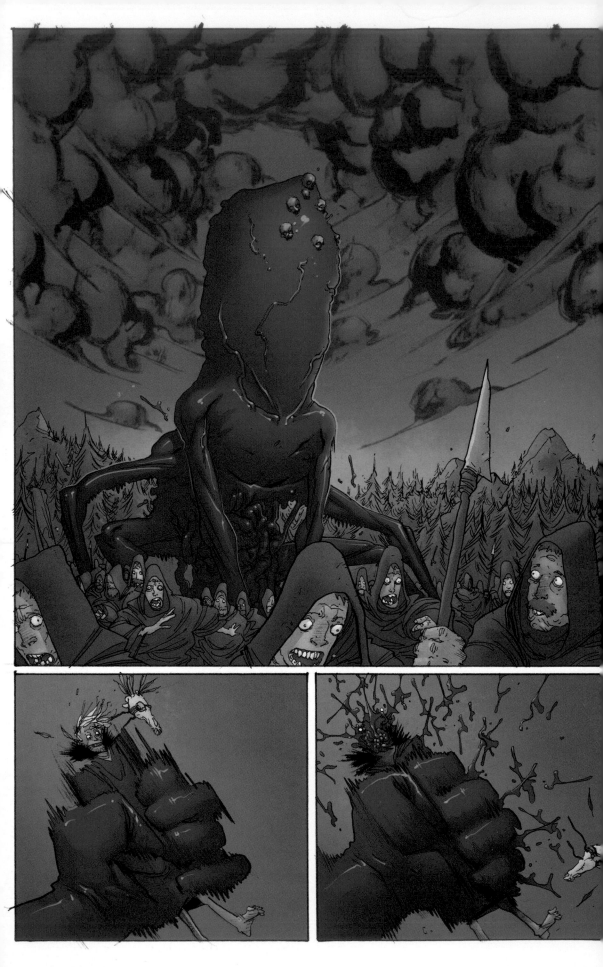

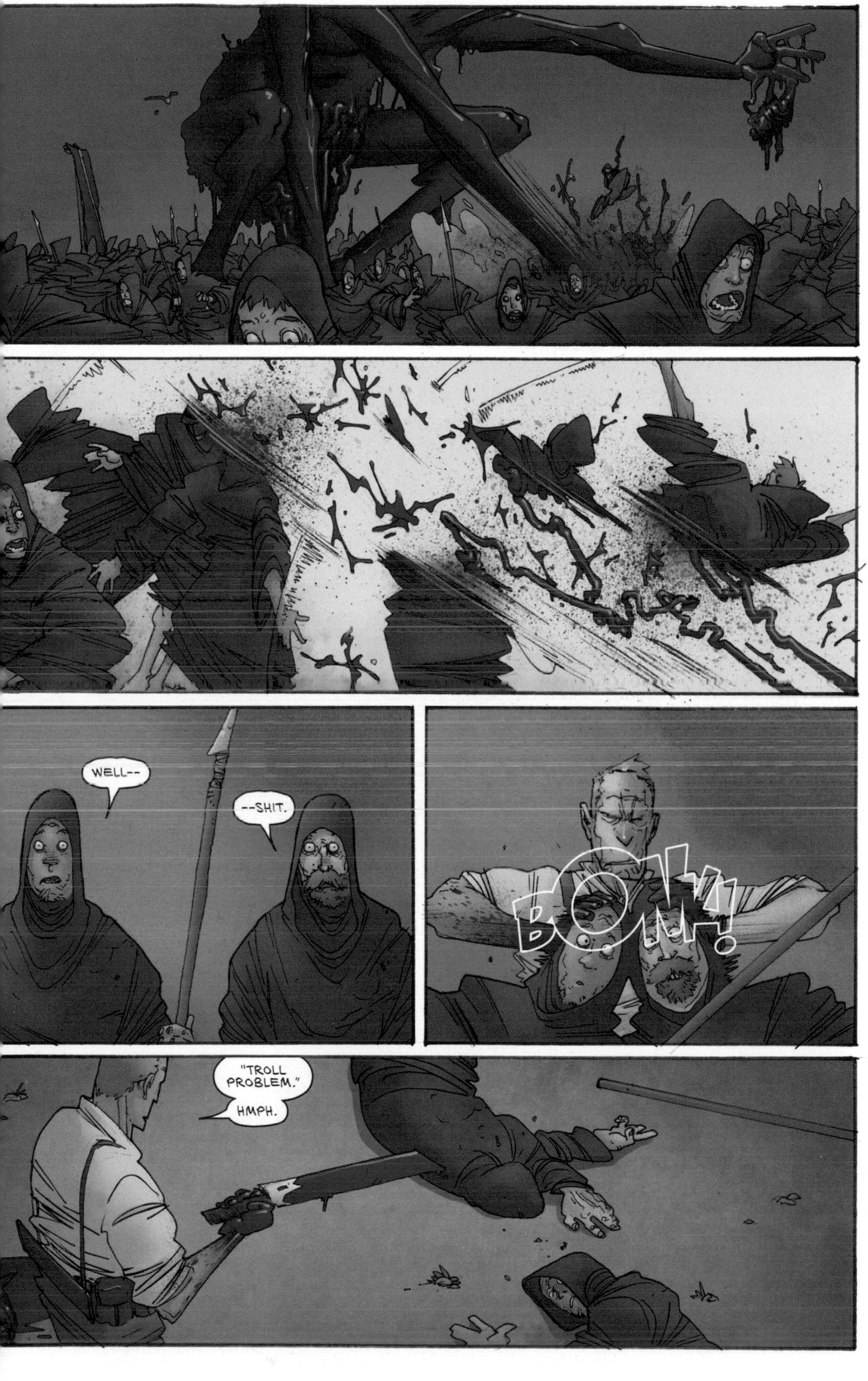
WELL--
--SHIT.
BONK!
"TROLL PROBLEM."
HMPH.

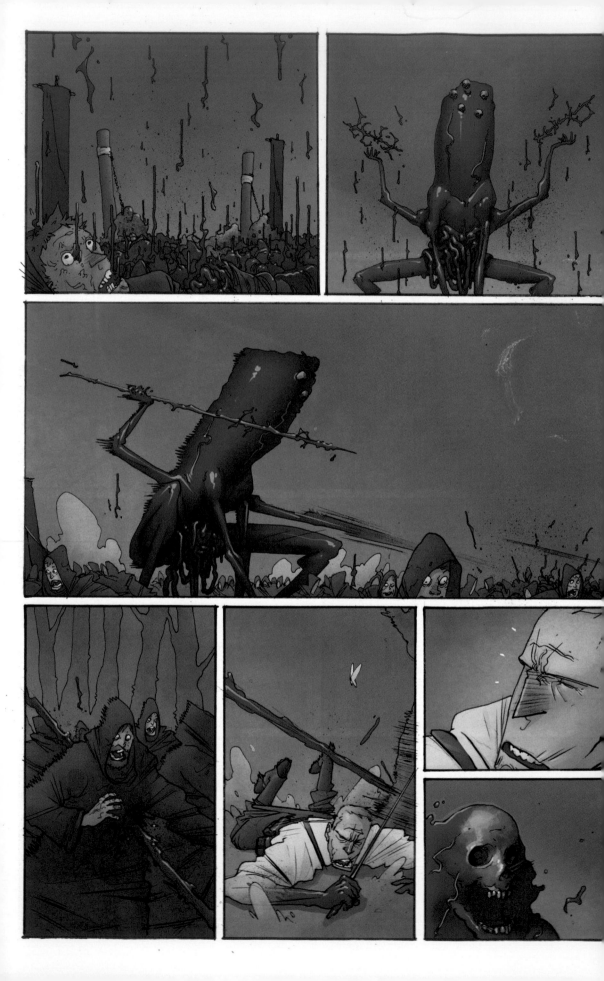

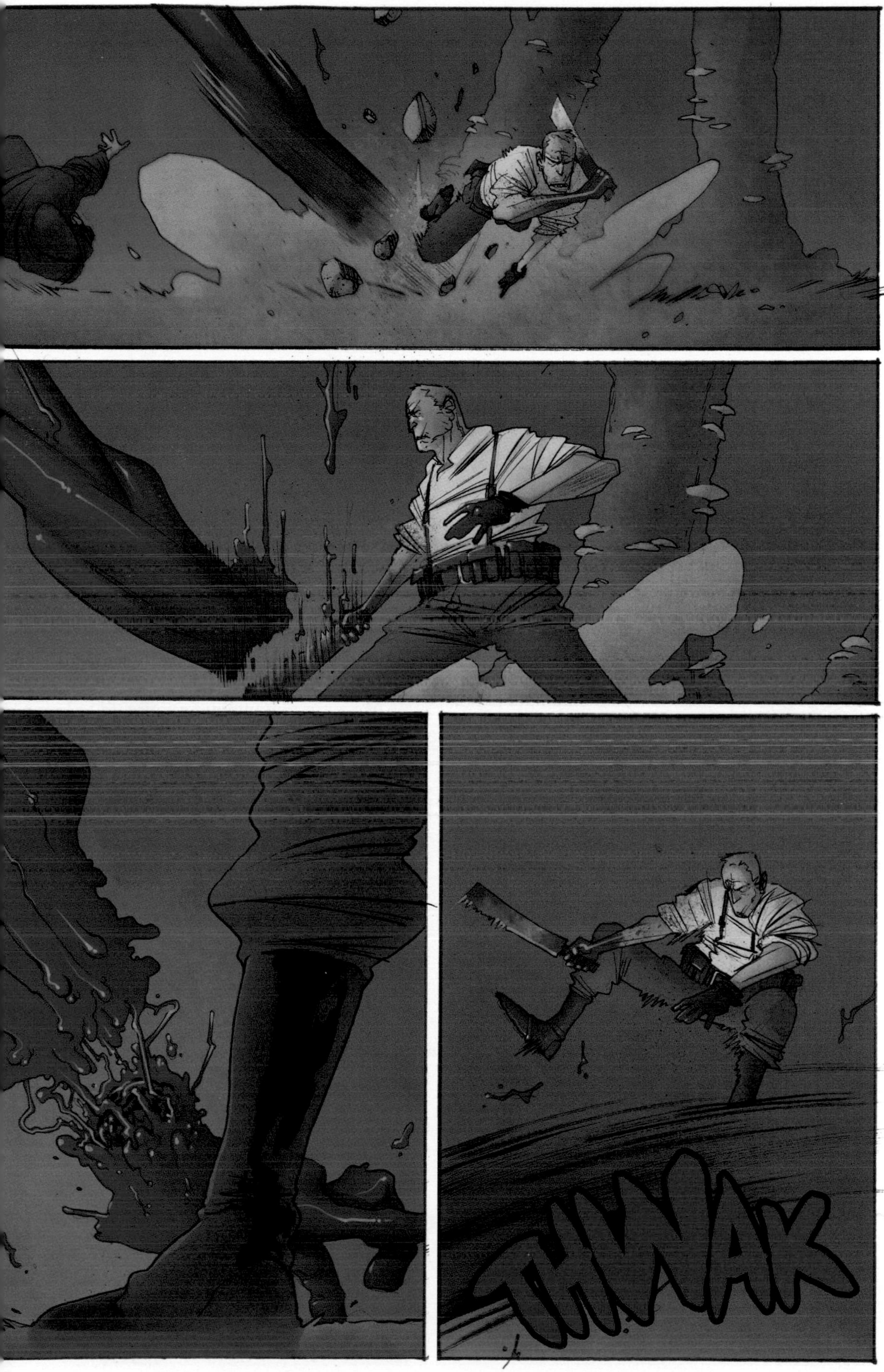
THWAK

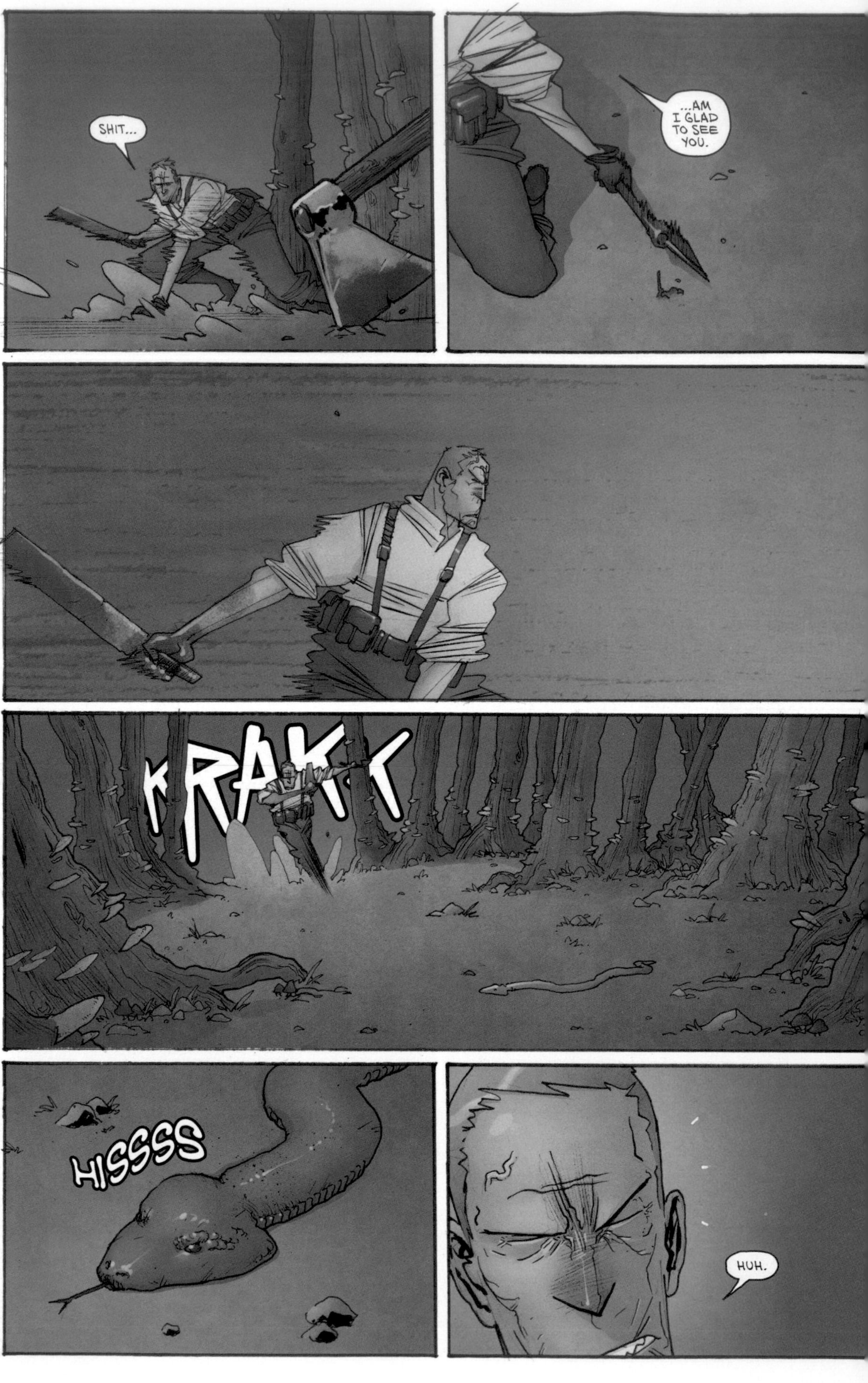
SHIT...
...AM I GLAD TO SEE YOU.
KRAKT
HISSSS
HUH.

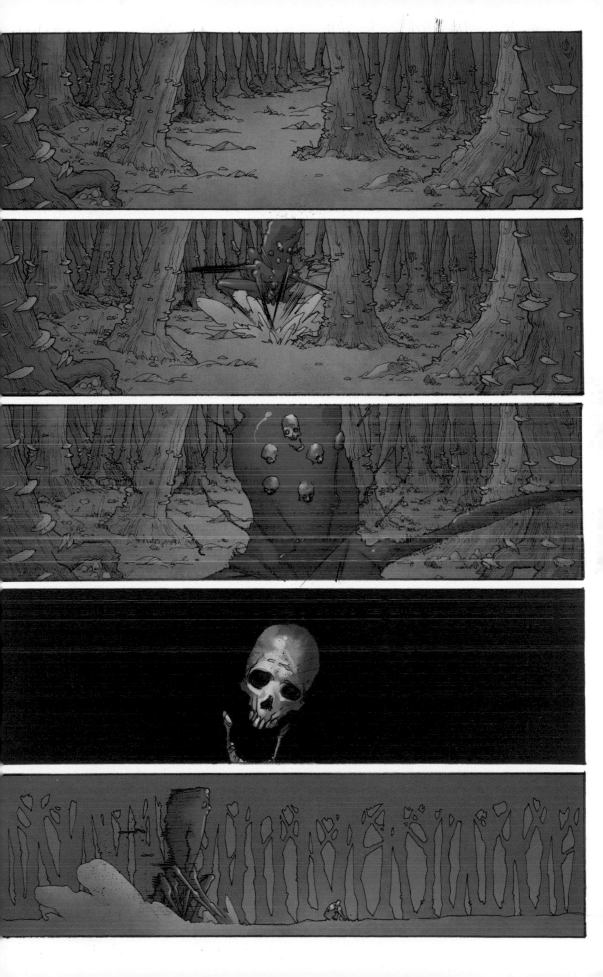

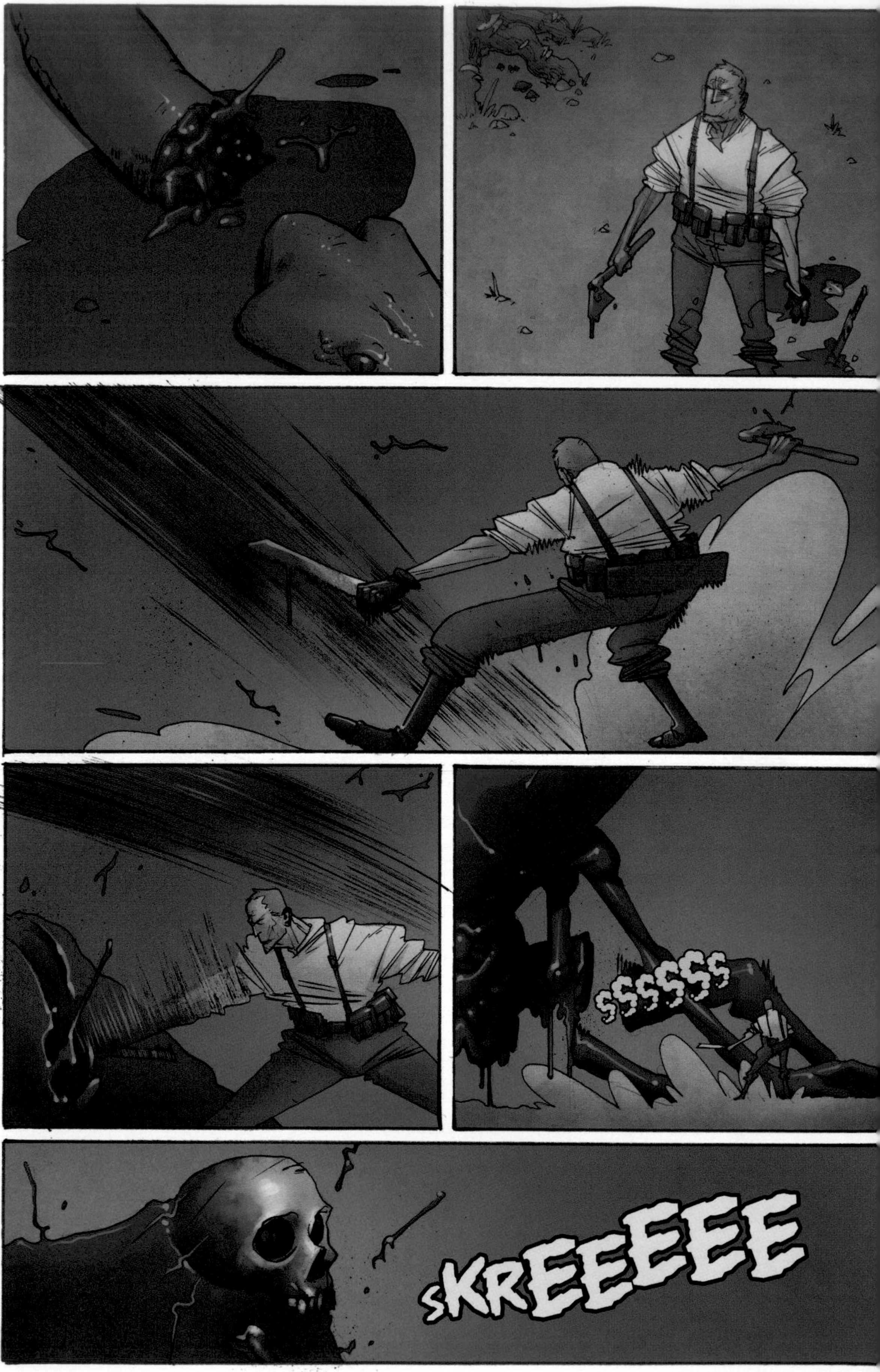
SSSSSS
sKREEEEEE

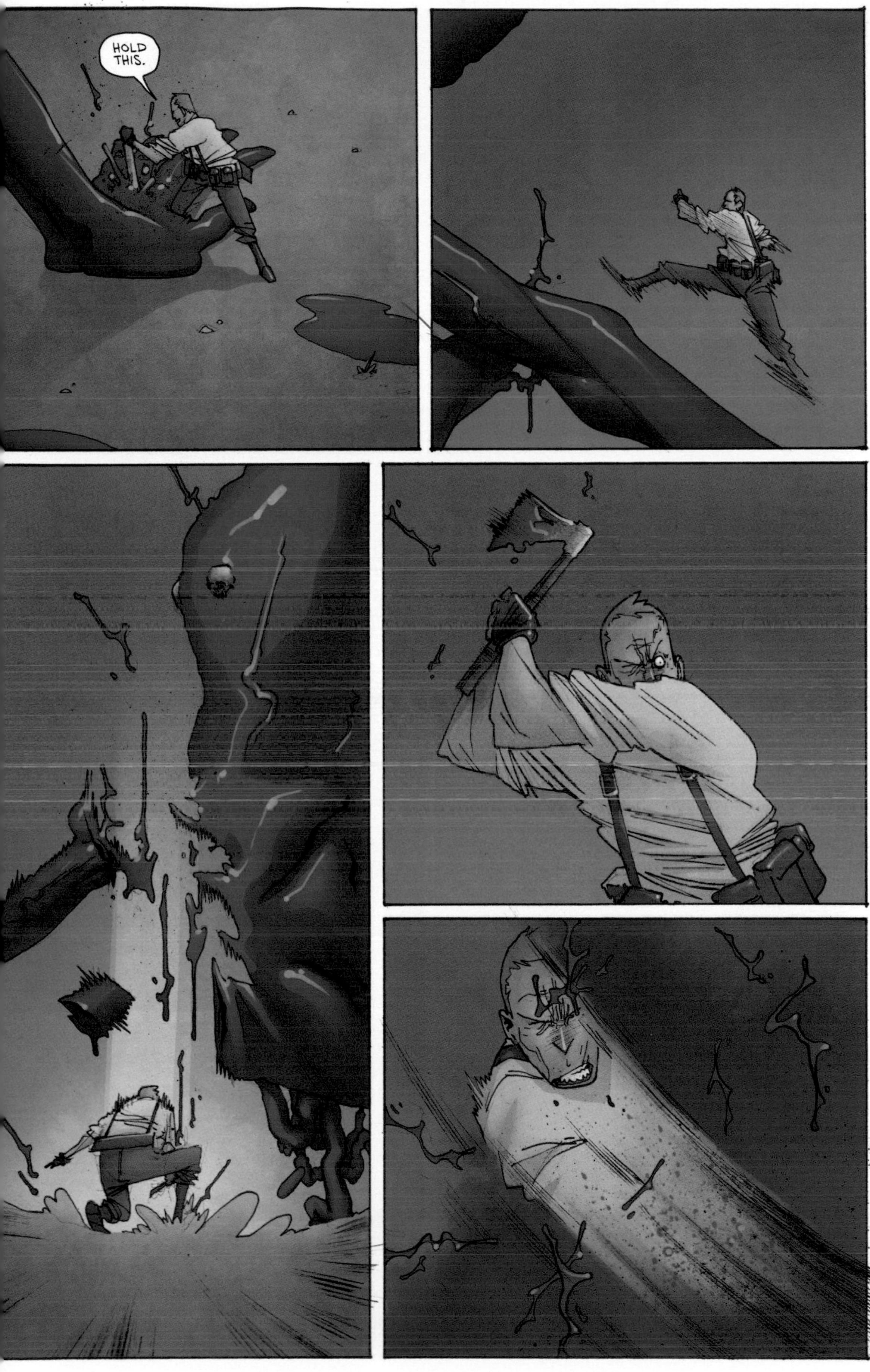
HOLD THIS.

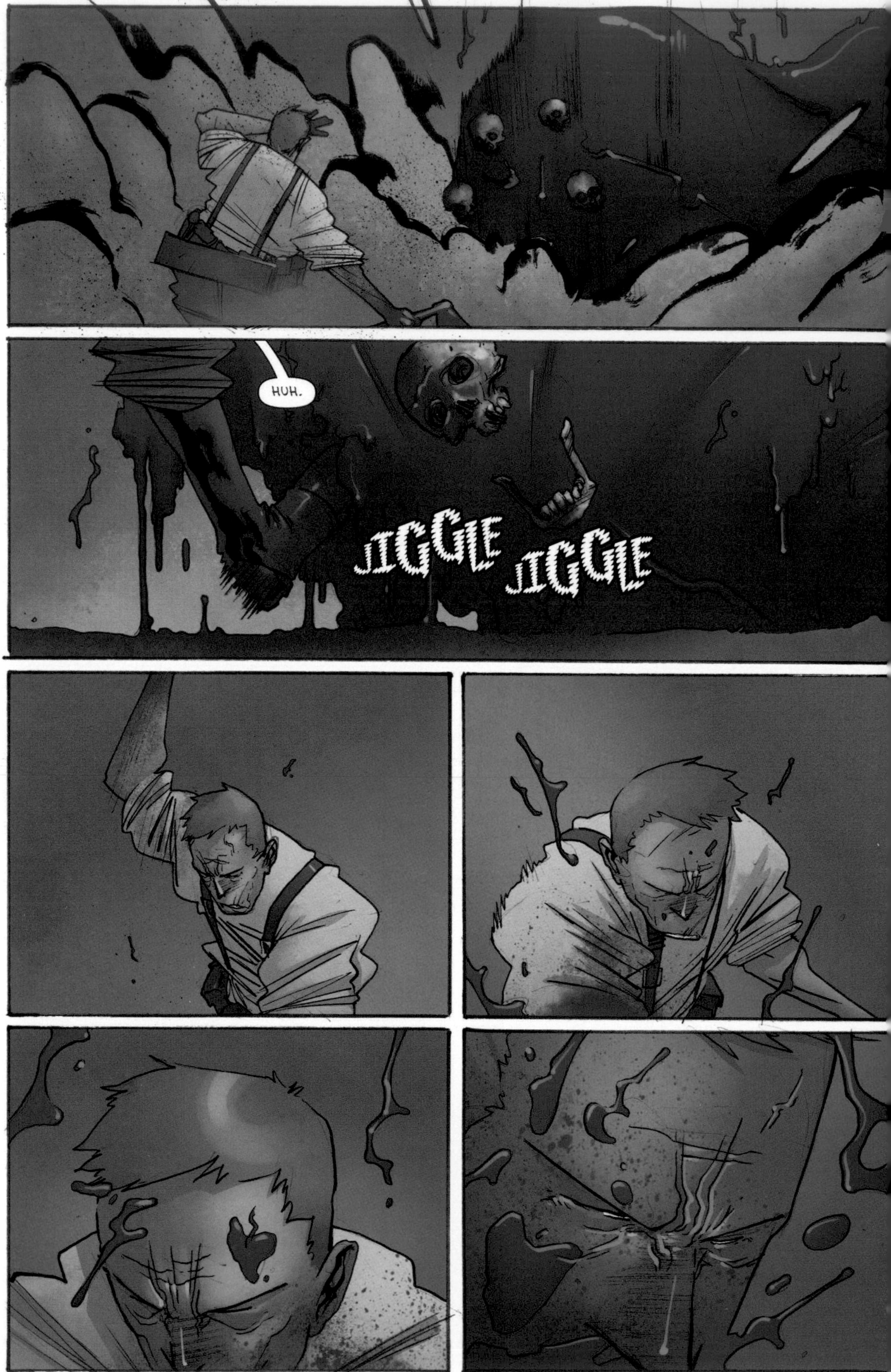
HUH.
JIGGLE JIGGLE

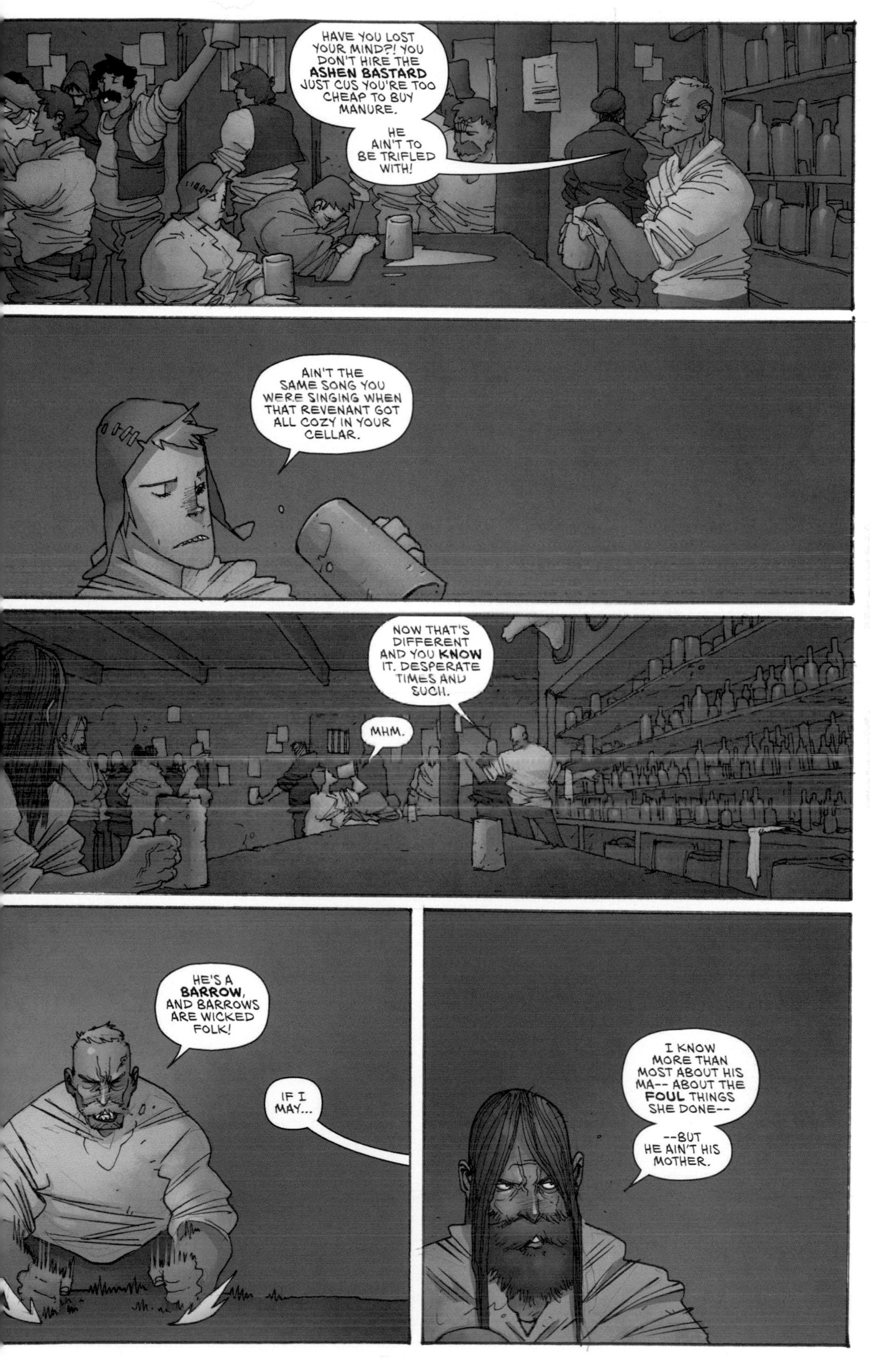
HAVE YOU LOST YOUR MIND?! YOU DON'T HIRE THE **ASHEN BASTARD** JUST CUS YOU'RE TOO CHEAP TO BUY MANURE.
HE AIN'T TO BE TRIFLED WITH!
AIN'T THE SAME SONG YOU WERE SINGING WHEN THAT REVENANT GOT ALL COZY IN YOUR CELLAR.
NOW THAT'S DIFFERENT AND YOU **KNOW** IT. DESPERATE TIMES AND SUCH.
MHM.
HE'S A **BARROW**, AND BARROWS ARE WICKED FOLK!
IF I MAY...
I KNOW MORE THAN MOST ABOUT HIS MA-- ABOUT THE **FOUL** THINGS SHE DONE--
--BUT HE AIN'T HIS MOTHER.

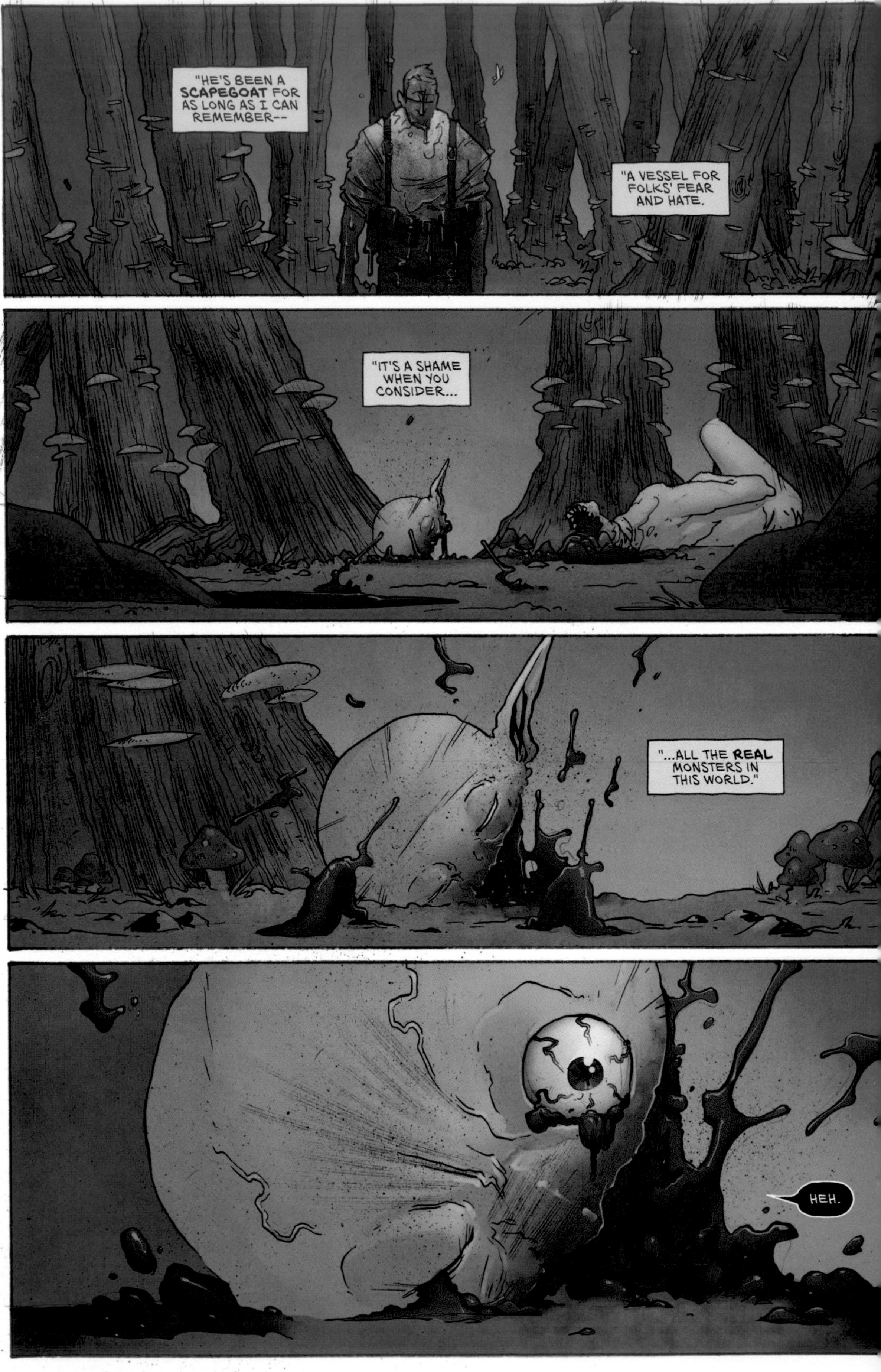
"HE'S BEEN A SCAPEGOAT FOR AS LONG AS I CAN REMEMBER--
"A VESSEL FOR FOLKS' FEAR AND HATE.
"IT'S A SHAME WHEN YOU CONSIDER...
"...ALL THE REAL MONSTERS IN THIS WORLD."
HEH.

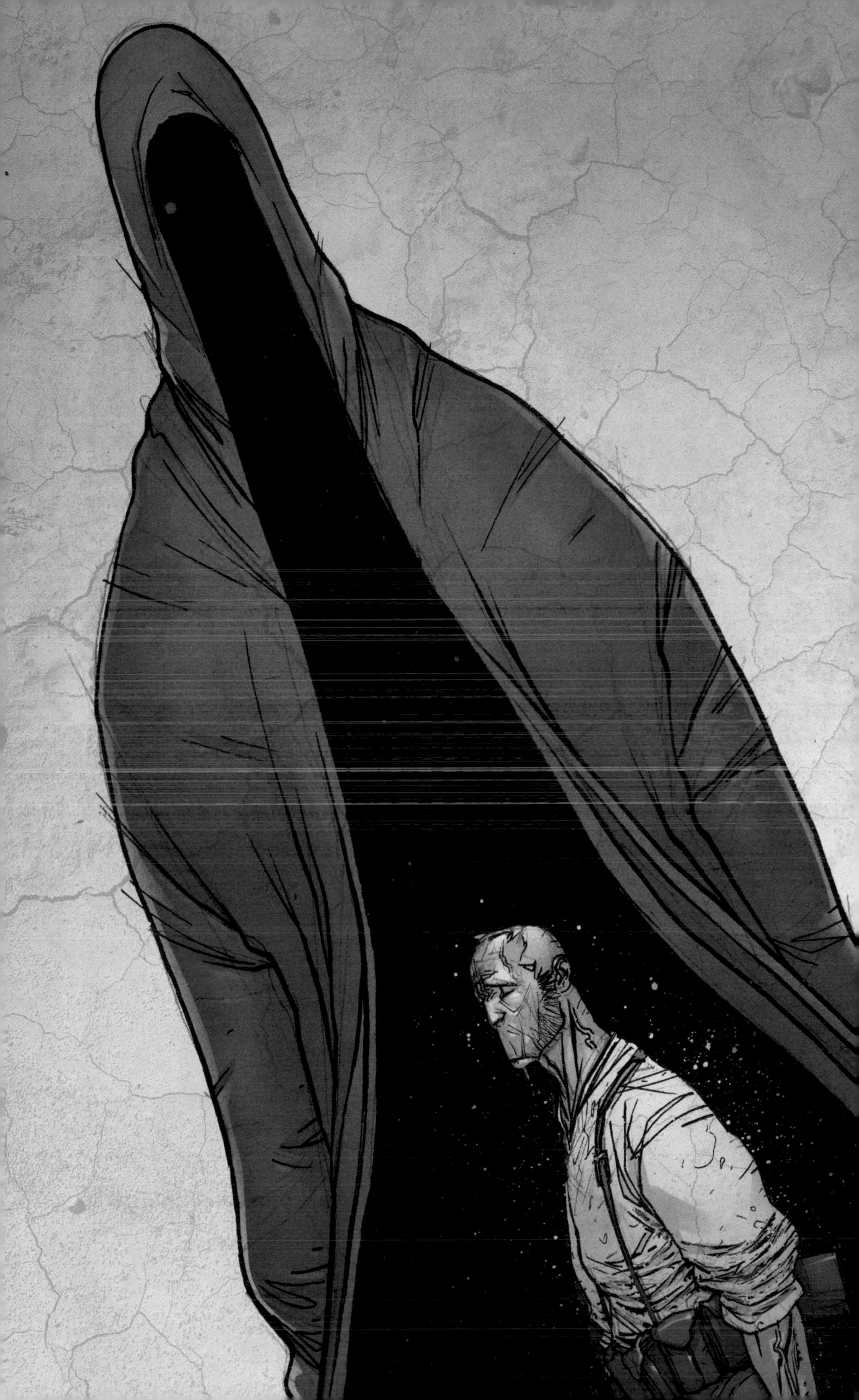

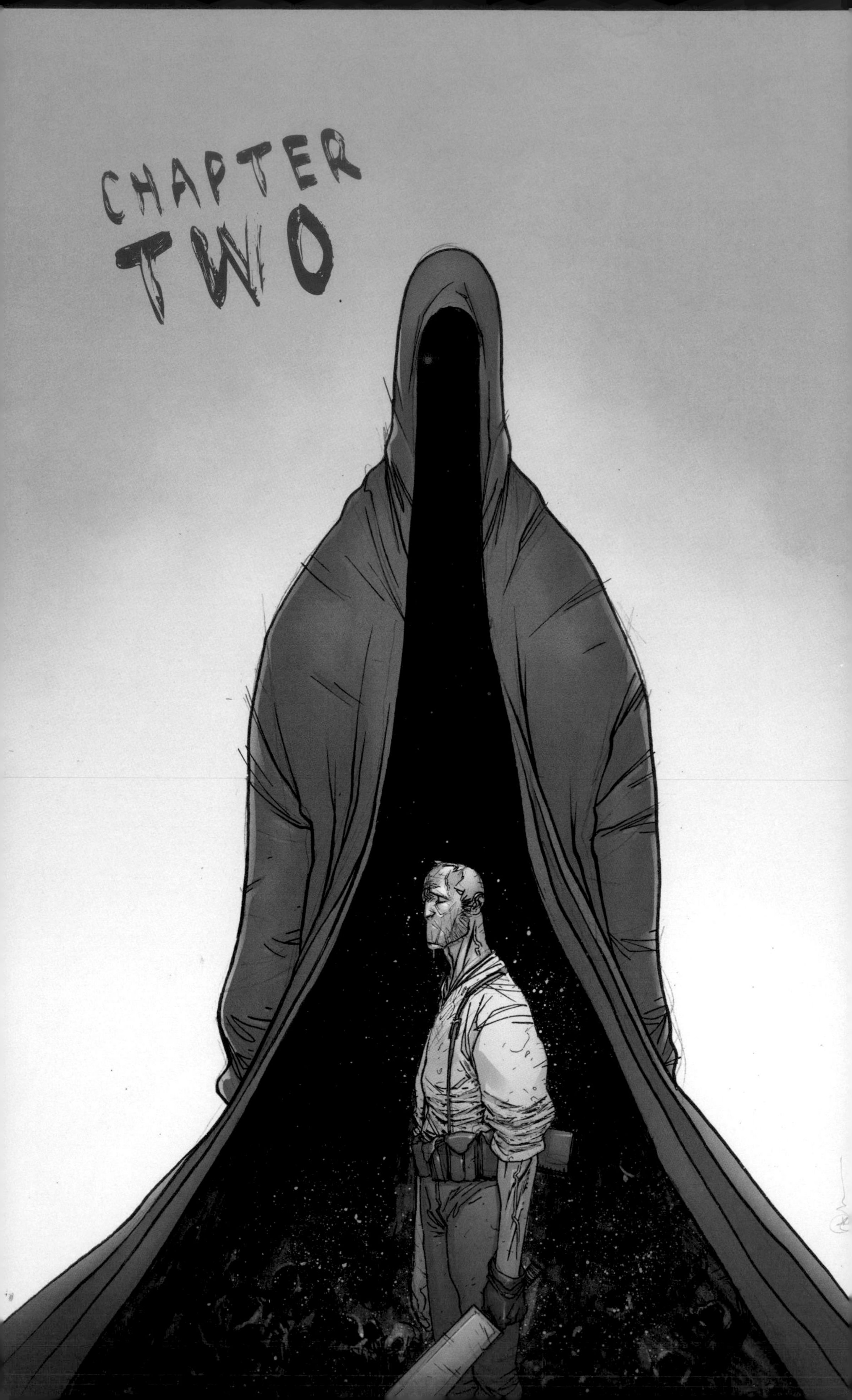
CHAPTER
TWO

THE
BLOOD-SOAKED
GROVE.

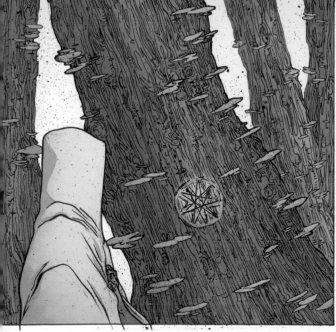

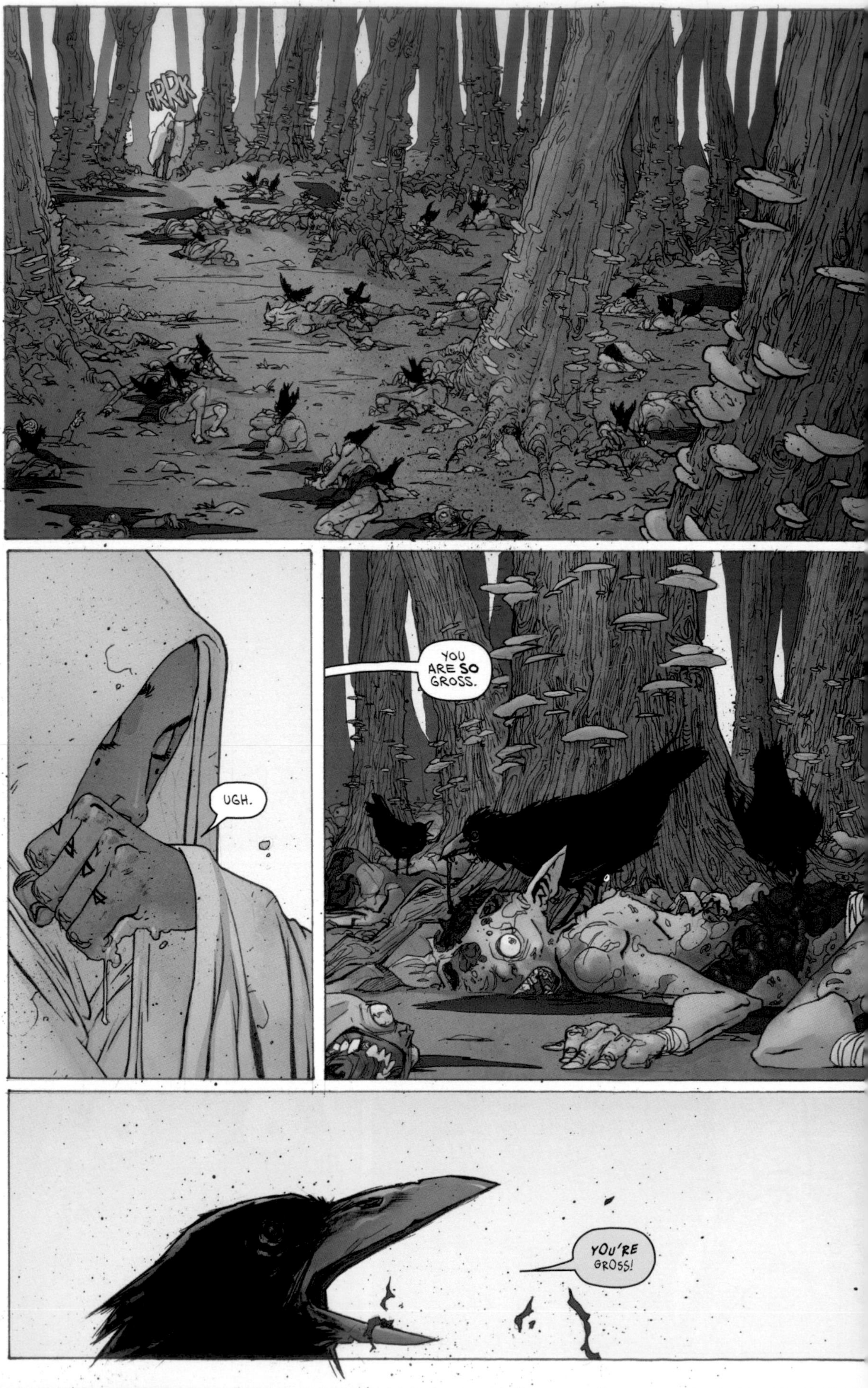
HRRK
UGH.
YOU ARE SO GROSS.
YOU'RE GROSS!

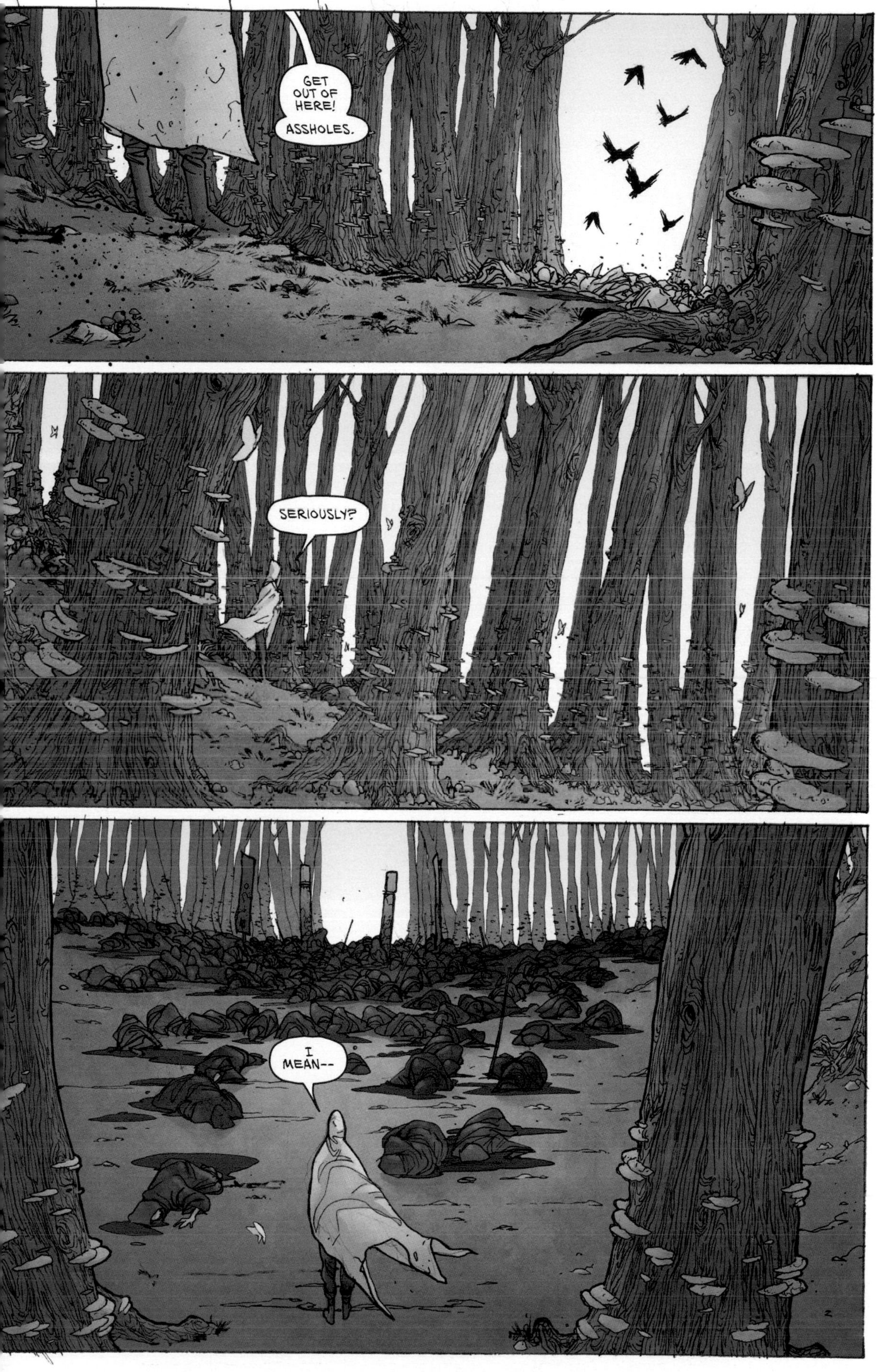

GET OUT OF HERE!
ASSHOLES.
SERIOUSLY?
I MEAN--

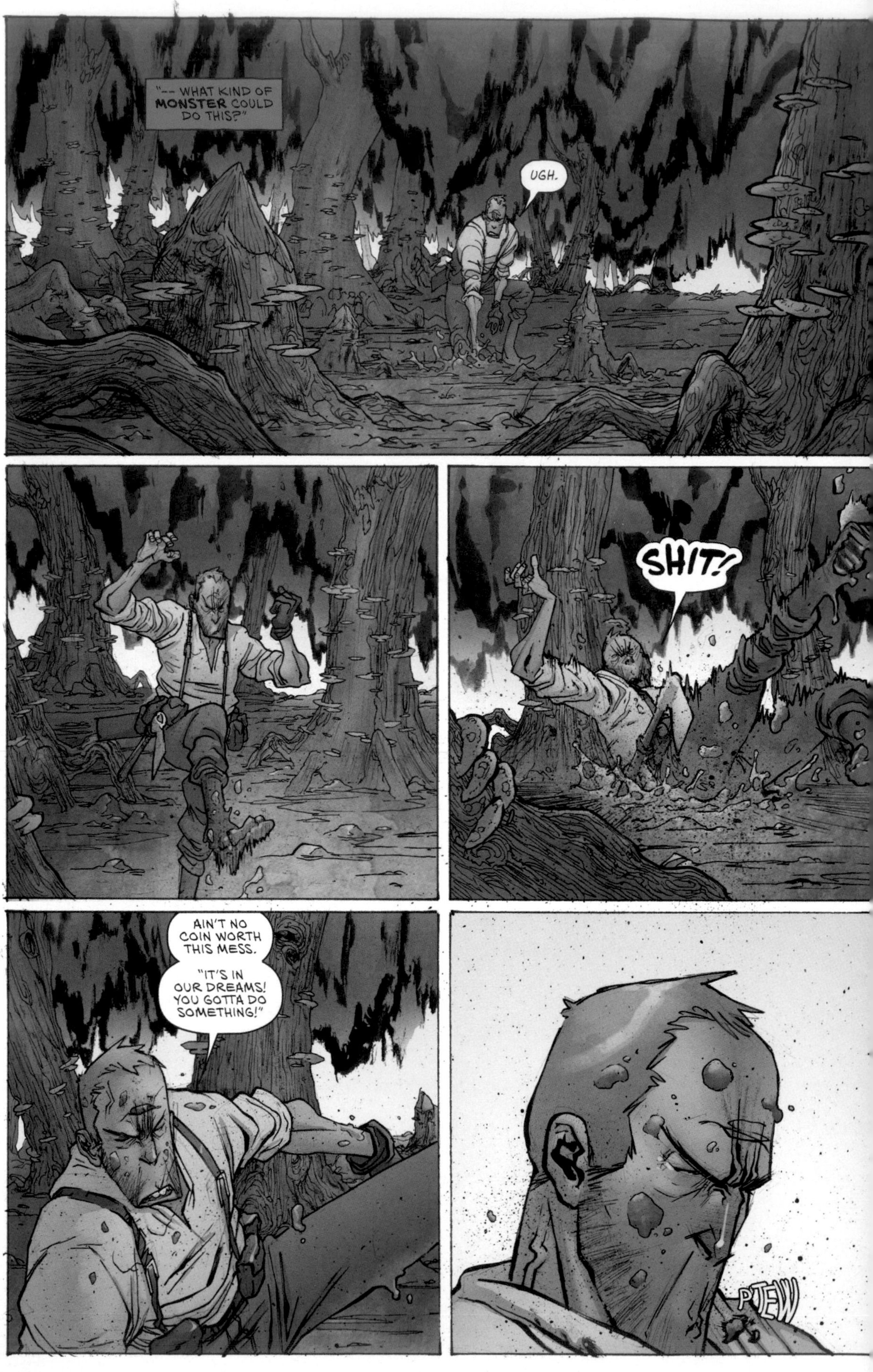
"-- WHAT KIND OF MONSTER COULD DO THIS?"
UGH.
SHIT!
AIN'T NO COIN WORTH THIS MESS.
"IT'S IN OUR DREAMS! YOU GOTTA DO SOMETHING!"
PTEW

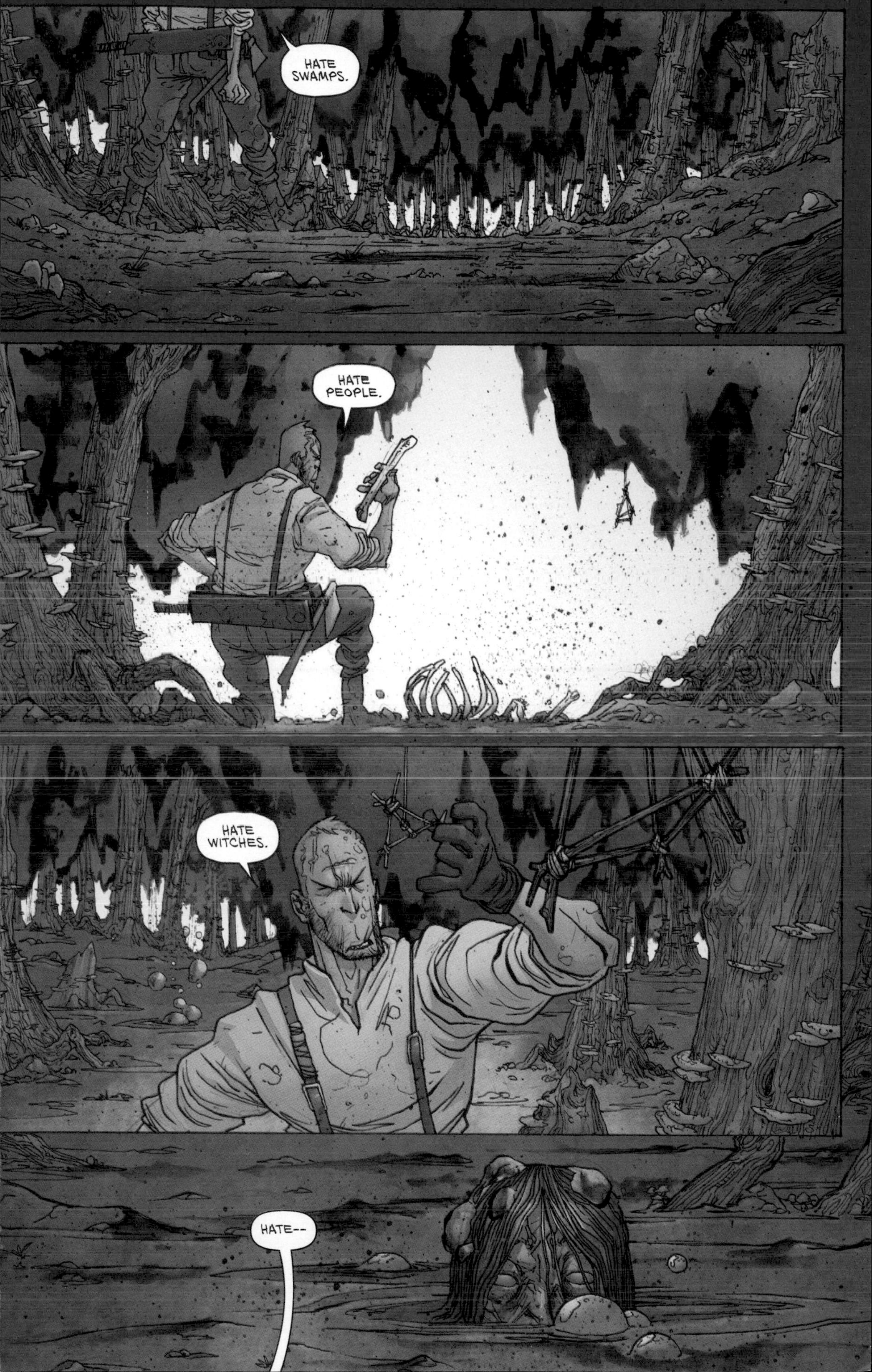
HATE SWAMPS.
HATE PEOPLE.
HATE WITCHES.
HATE--

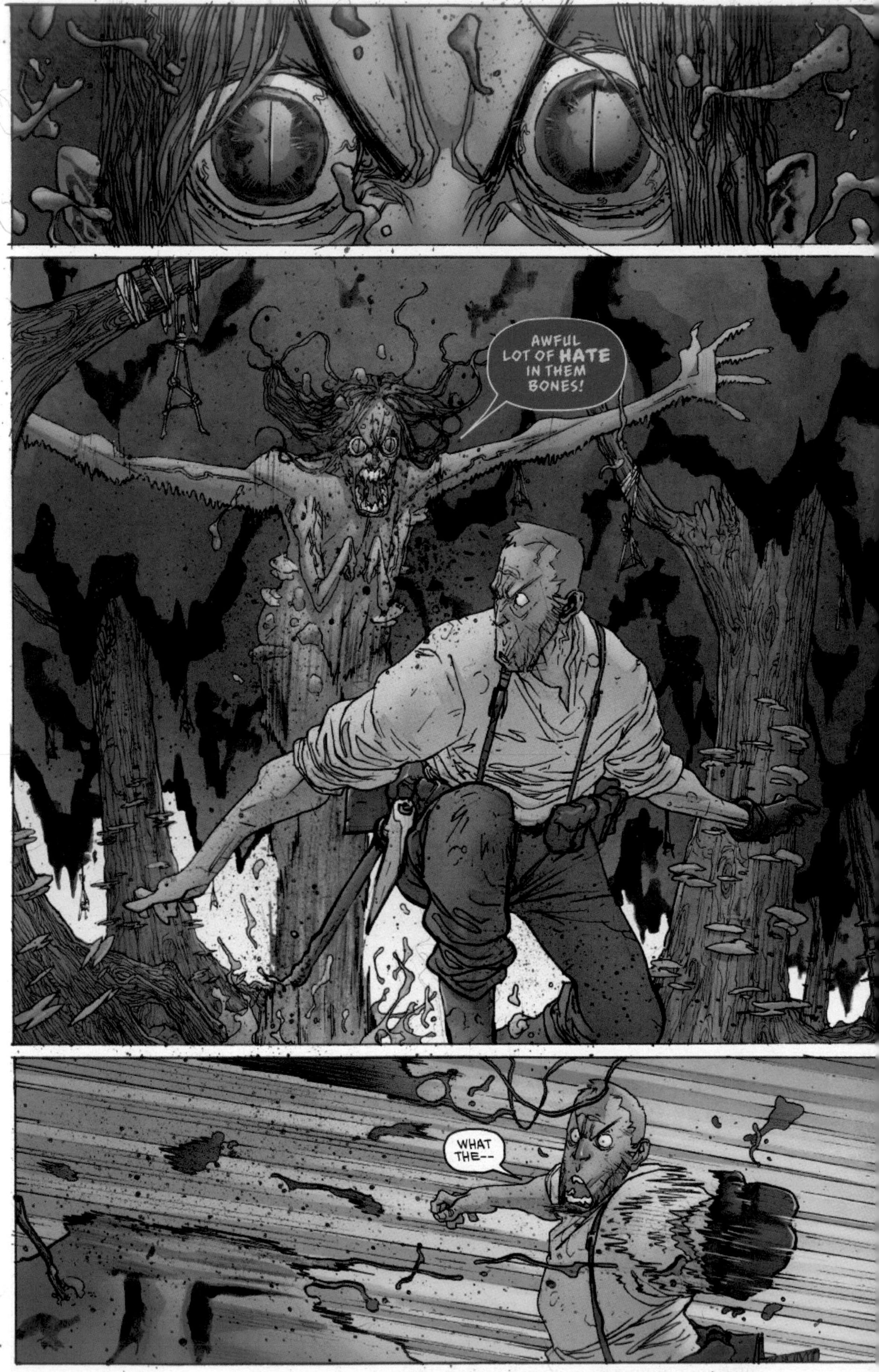
AWFUL LOT OF HATE IN THEM BONES!
WHAT THE--

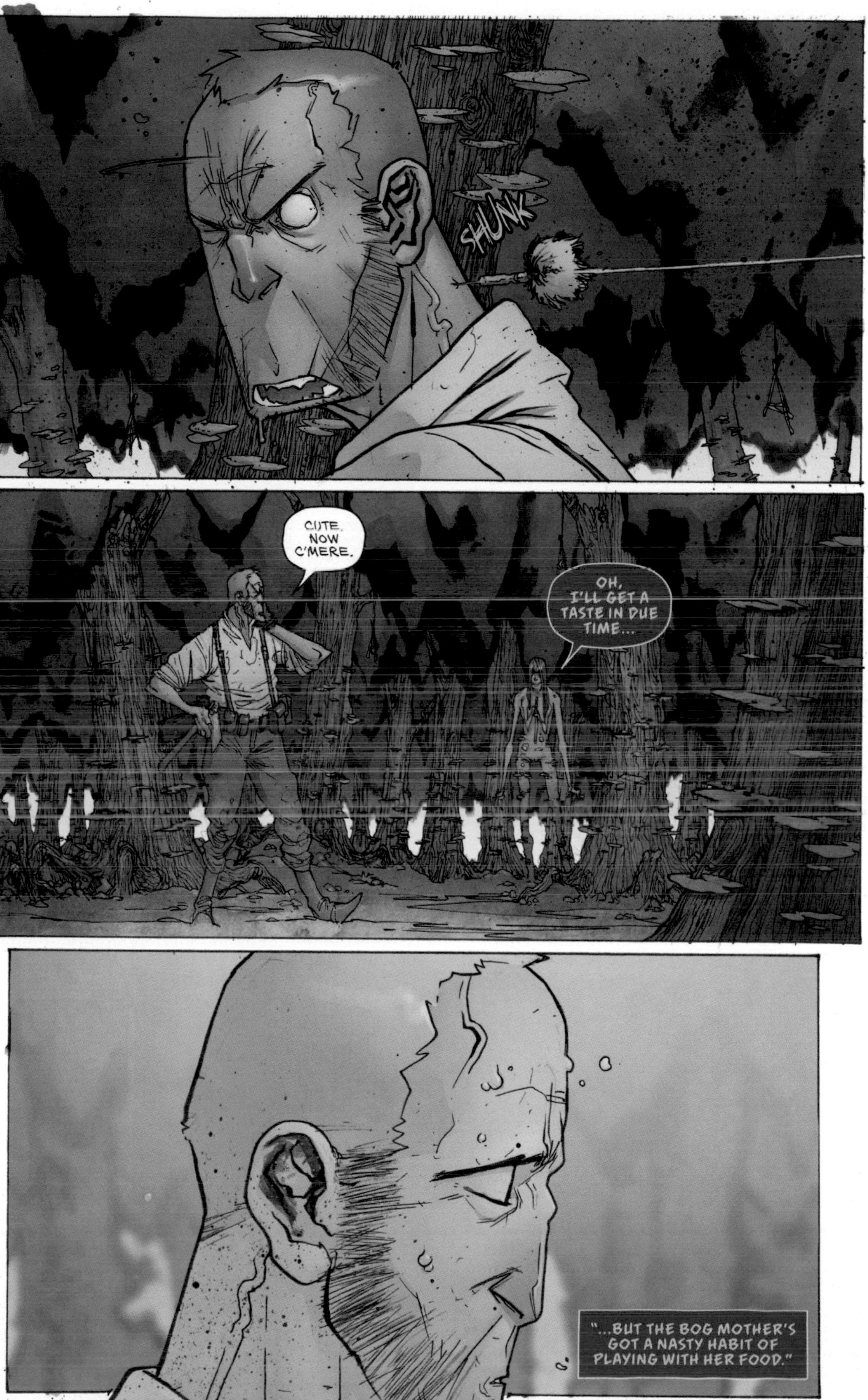
SHUNK
CUTE. NOW C'MERE.
OH, I'LL GET A TASTE IN DUE TIME...
"...BUT THE BOG MOTHER'S GOT A NASTY HABIT OF PLAYING WITH HER FOOD."

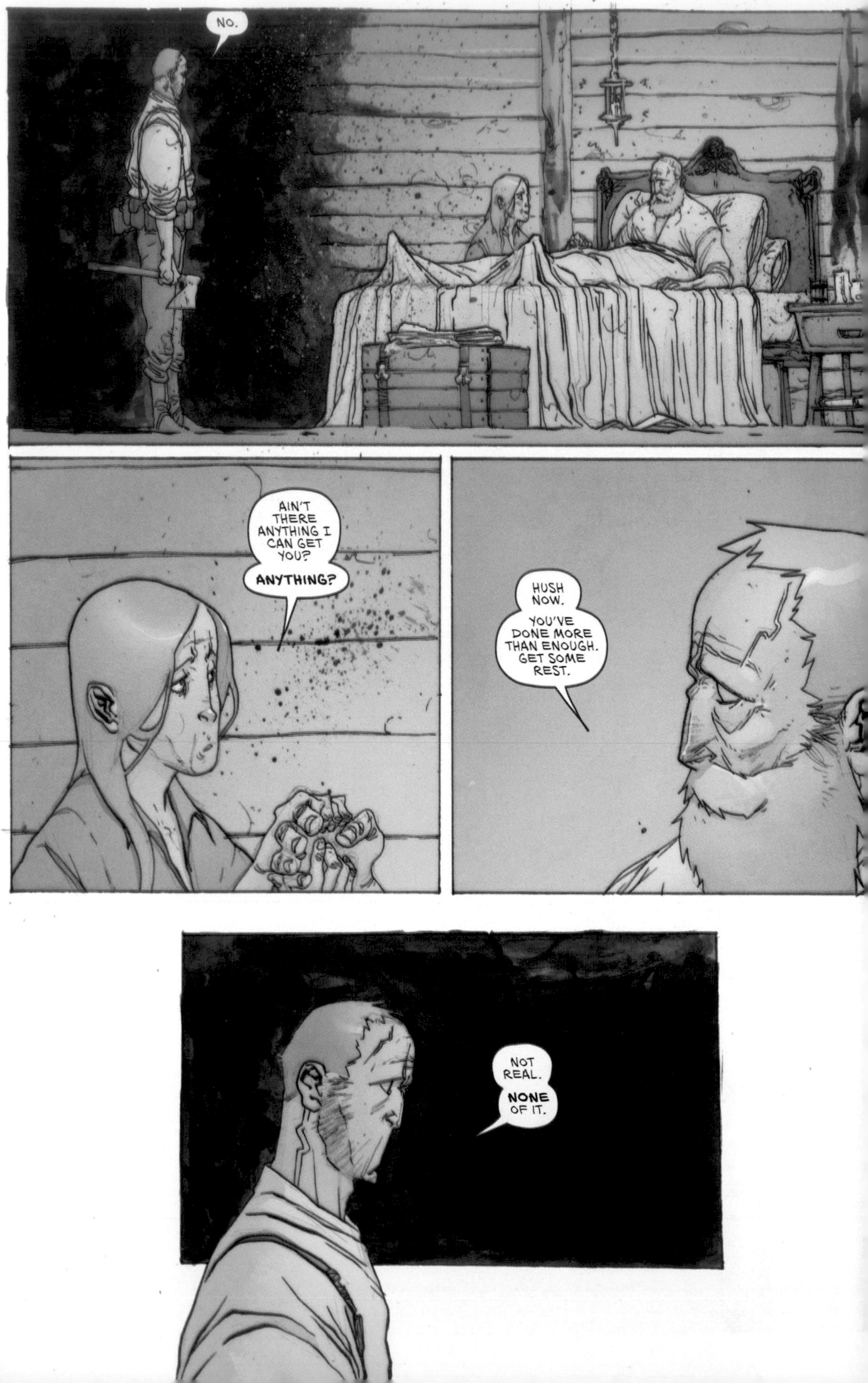
NO.
AIN'T THERE ANYTHING I CAN GET YOU?
ANYTHING?
HUSH NOW.
YOU'VE DONE MORE THAN ENOUGH. GET SOME REST.
NOT REAL.
NONE OF IT.

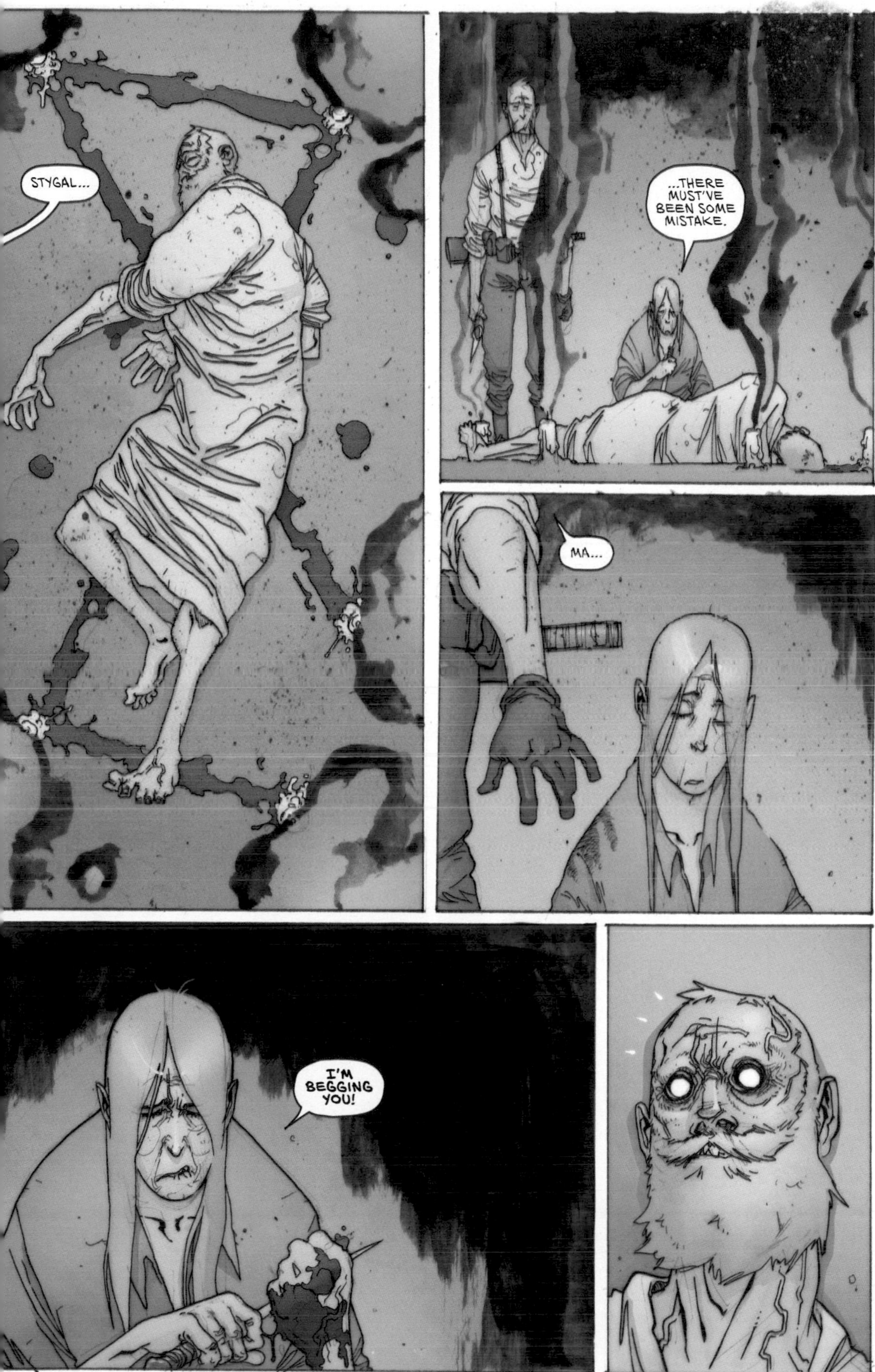
STYGAL...
...THERE MUST'VE BEEN SOME MISTAKE.
MA...
I'M BEGGING YOU!

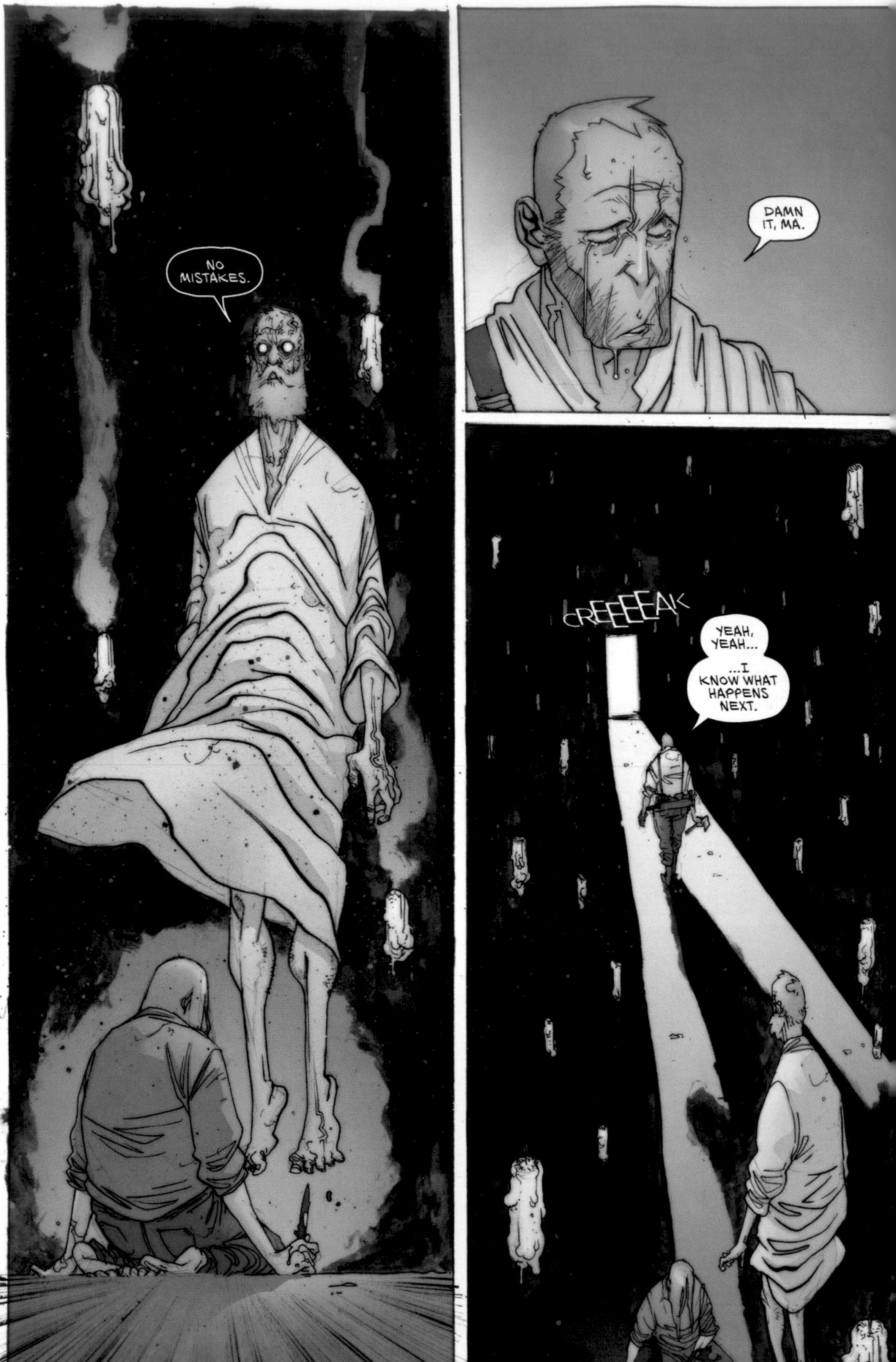
NO MISTAKES.
DAMN IT, MA.
CREEEEAK
YEAH, YEAH...
...I KNOW WHAT HAPPENS NEXT.

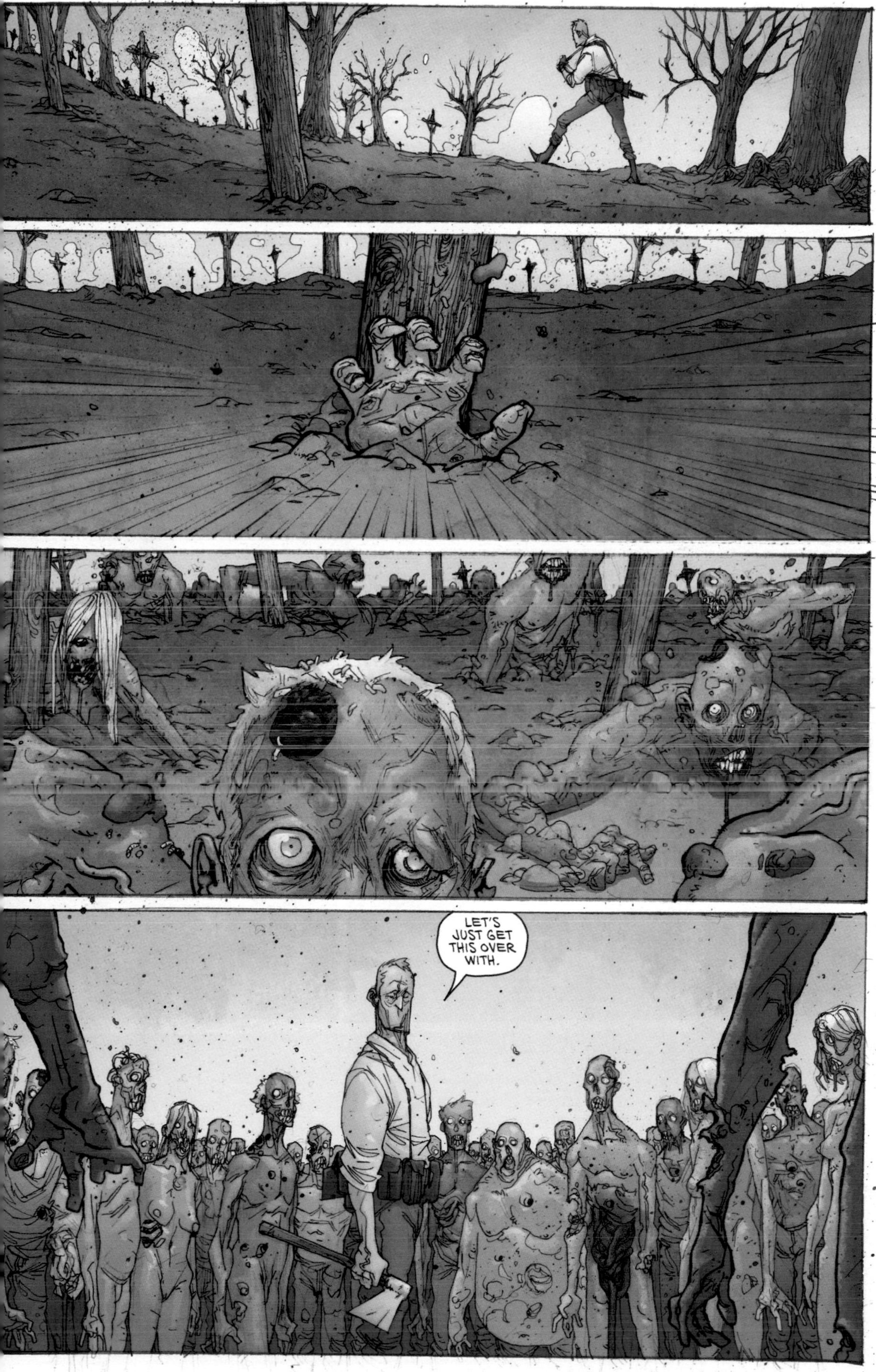
LET'S JUST GET THIS OVER WITH.

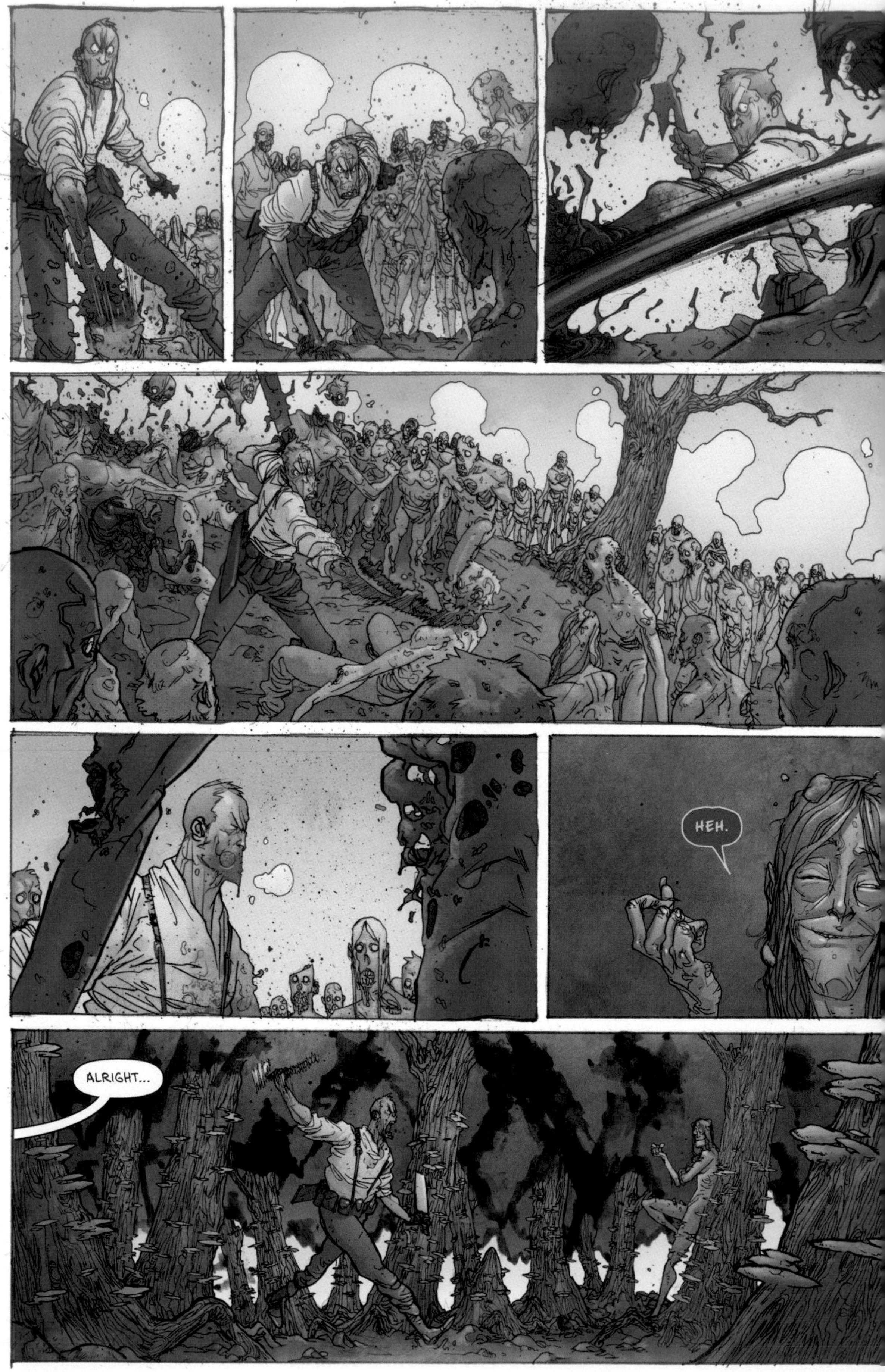
HEH.
ALRIGHT...

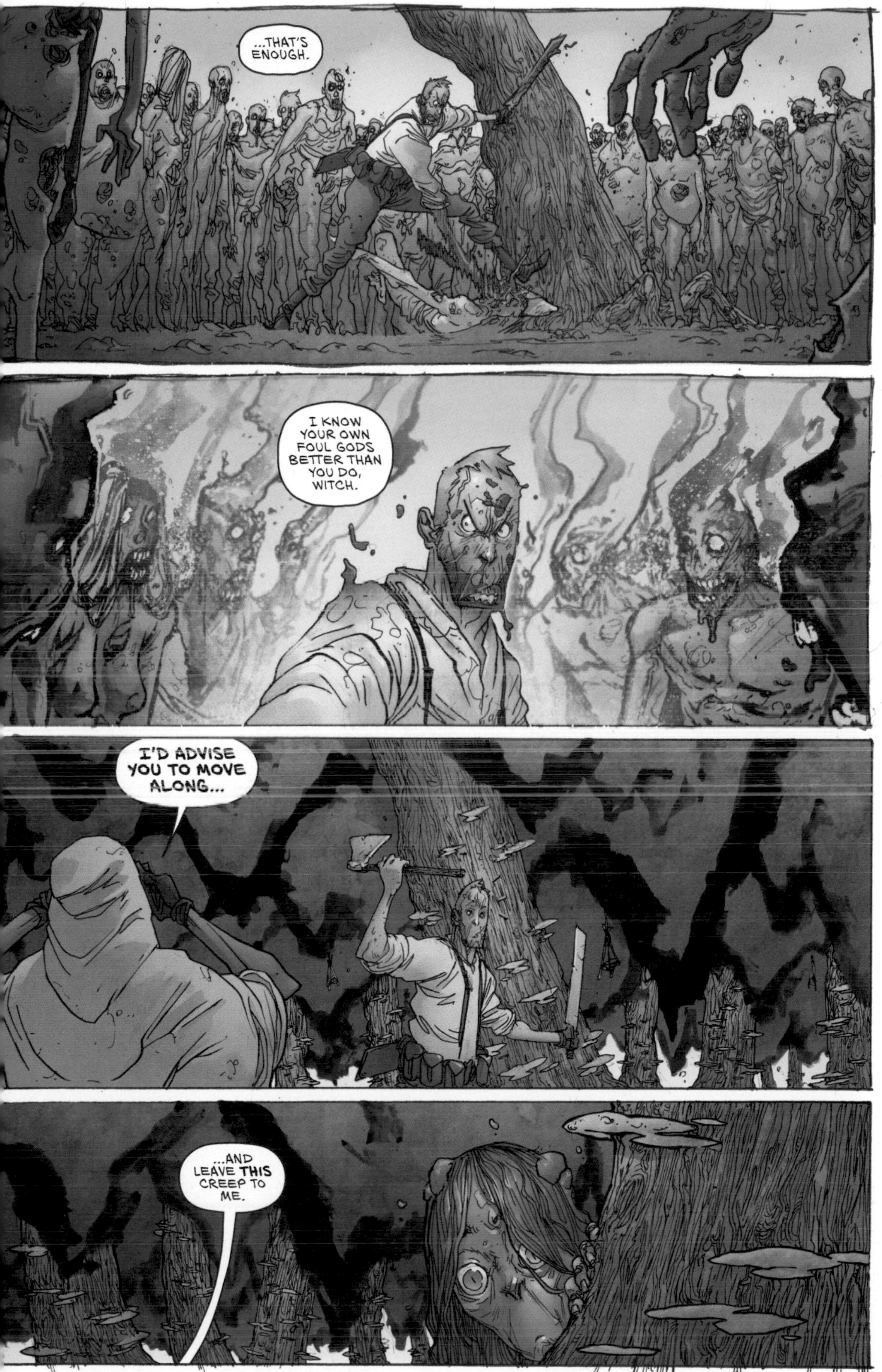
...THAT'S ENOUGH.
I KNOW YOUR OWN FOUL GODS BETTER THAN YOU DO, WITCH.
I'D ADVISE YOU TO MOVE ALONG...
...AND LEAVE THIS CREEP TO ME.

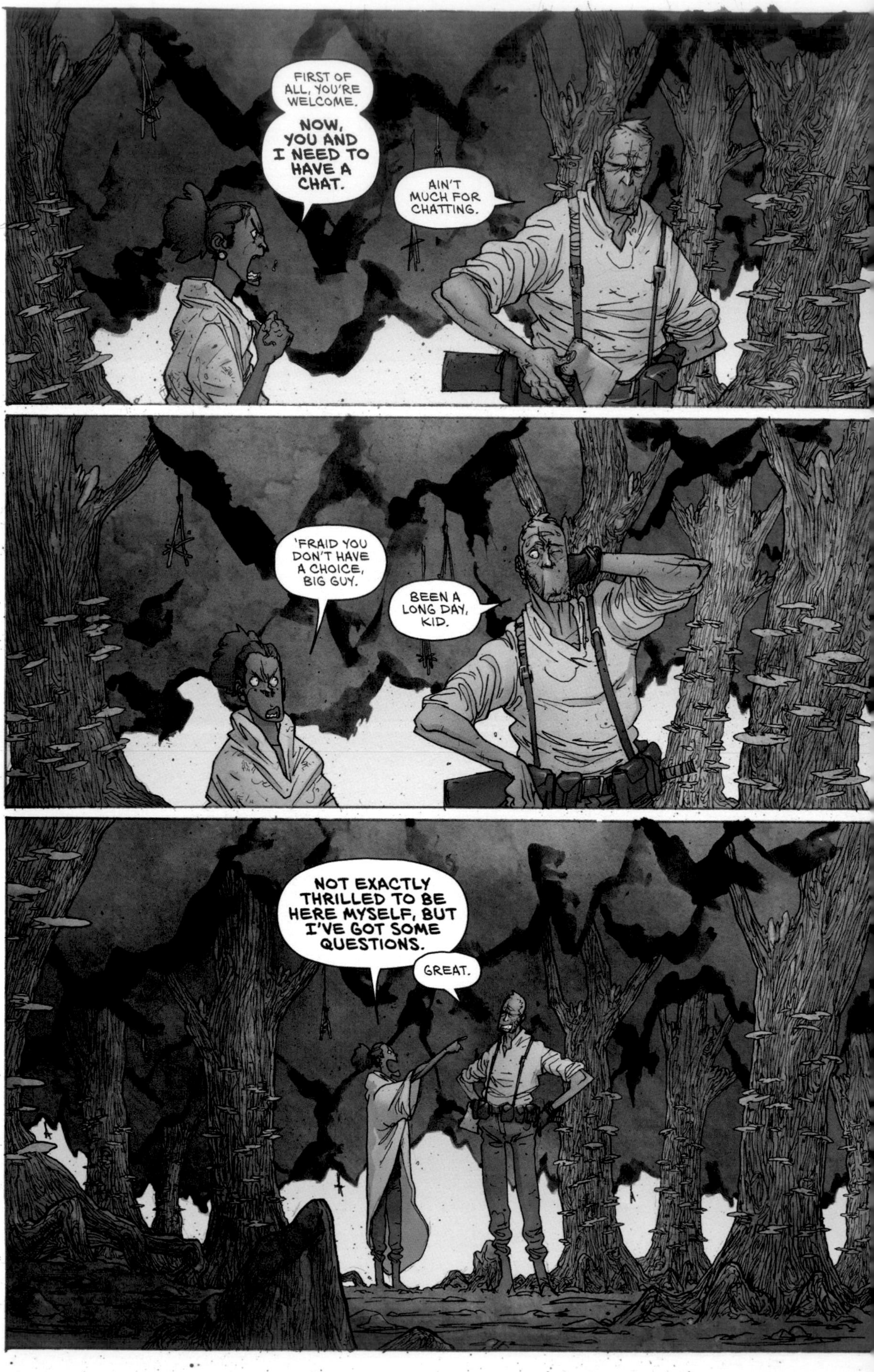
FIRST OF ALL, YOU'RE WELCOME.
NOW, YOU AND I NEED TO HAVE A CHAT.
AIN'T MUCH FOR CHATTING.
'FRAID YOU DON'T HAVE A CHOICE, BIG GUY.
BEEN A LONG DAY, KID.
NOT EXACTLY THRILLED TO BE HERE MYSELF, BUT I'VE GOT SOME QUESTIONS.
GREAT.

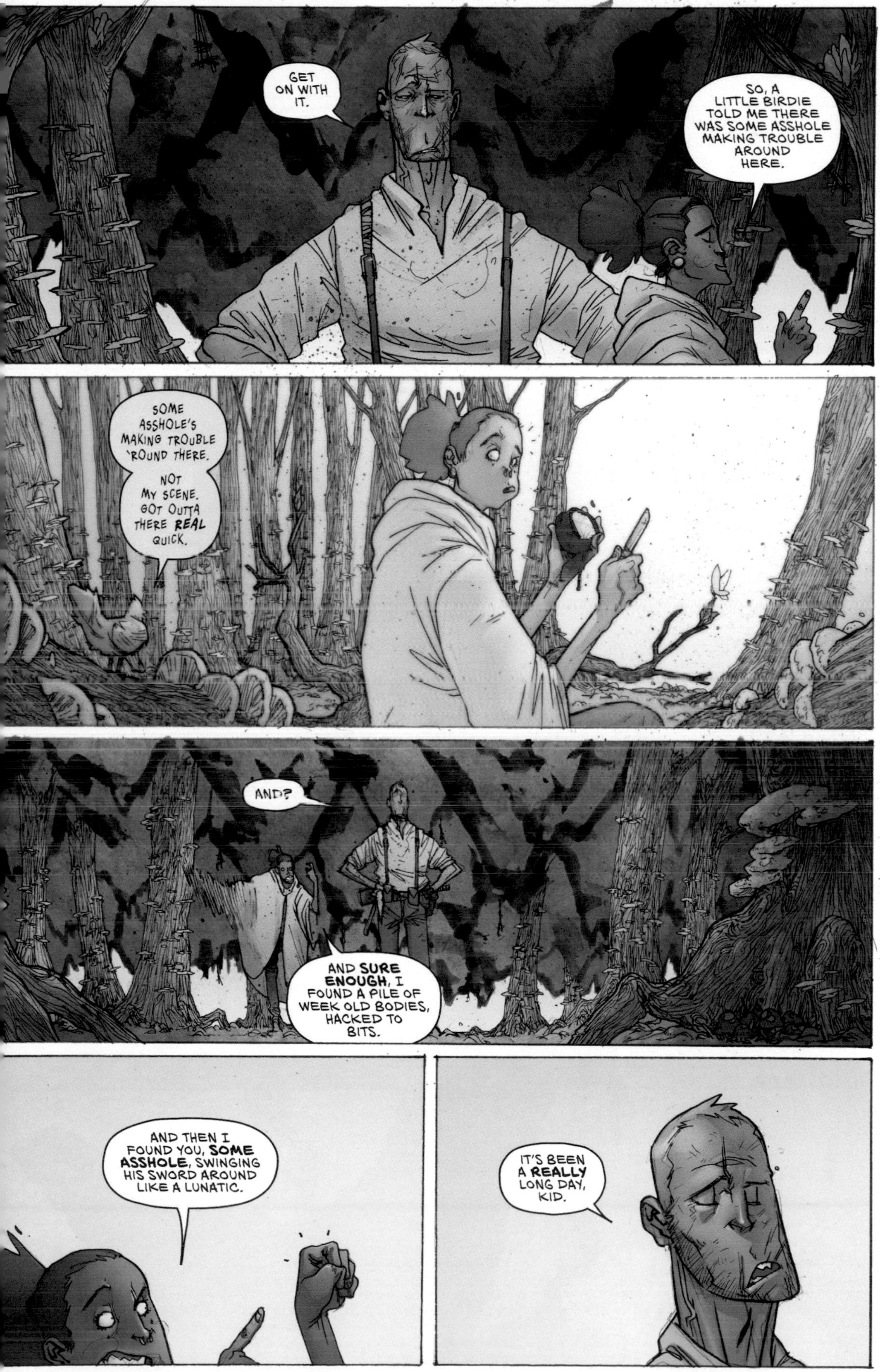
GET ON WITH IT.
SO, A LITTLE BIRDIE TOLD ME THERE WAS SOME ASSHOLE MAKING TROUBLE AROUND HERE.
SOME ASSHOLE'S MAKING TROUBLE 'ROUND THERE.
NOT MY SCENE. GOT OUTTA THERE **REAL** QUICK.
AND?
AND **SURE ENOUGH,** I FOUND A PILE OF WEEK OLD BODIES, HACKED TO BITS.
AND THEN I FOUND YOU, **SOME ASSHOLE,** SWINGING HIS SWORD AROUND LIKE A LUNATIC.
IT'S BEEN A **REALLY** LONG DAY, KID.

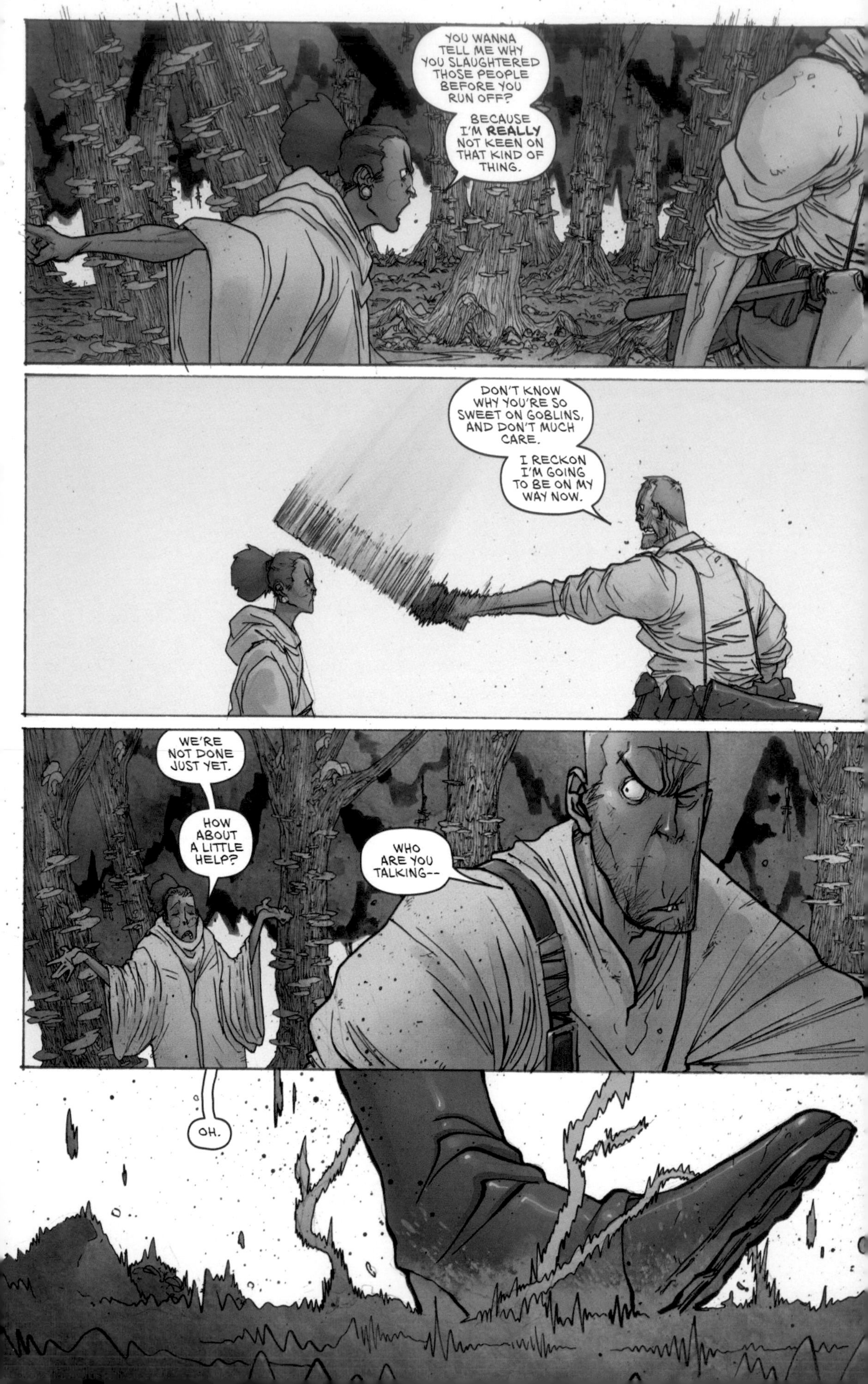
YOU WANNA TELL ME WHY YOU SLAUGHTERED THOSE PEOPLE BEFORE YOU RUN OFF?
BECAUSE I'M **REALLY** NOT KEEN ON THAT KIND OF THING.
DON'T KNOW WHY YOU'RE SO SWEET ON GOBLINS, AND DON'T MUCH CARE.
I RECKON I'M GOING TO BE ON MY WAY NOW.
WE'RE NOT DONE JUST YET.
HOW ABOUT A LITTLE HELP?
WHO ARE YOU TALKING--
OH.

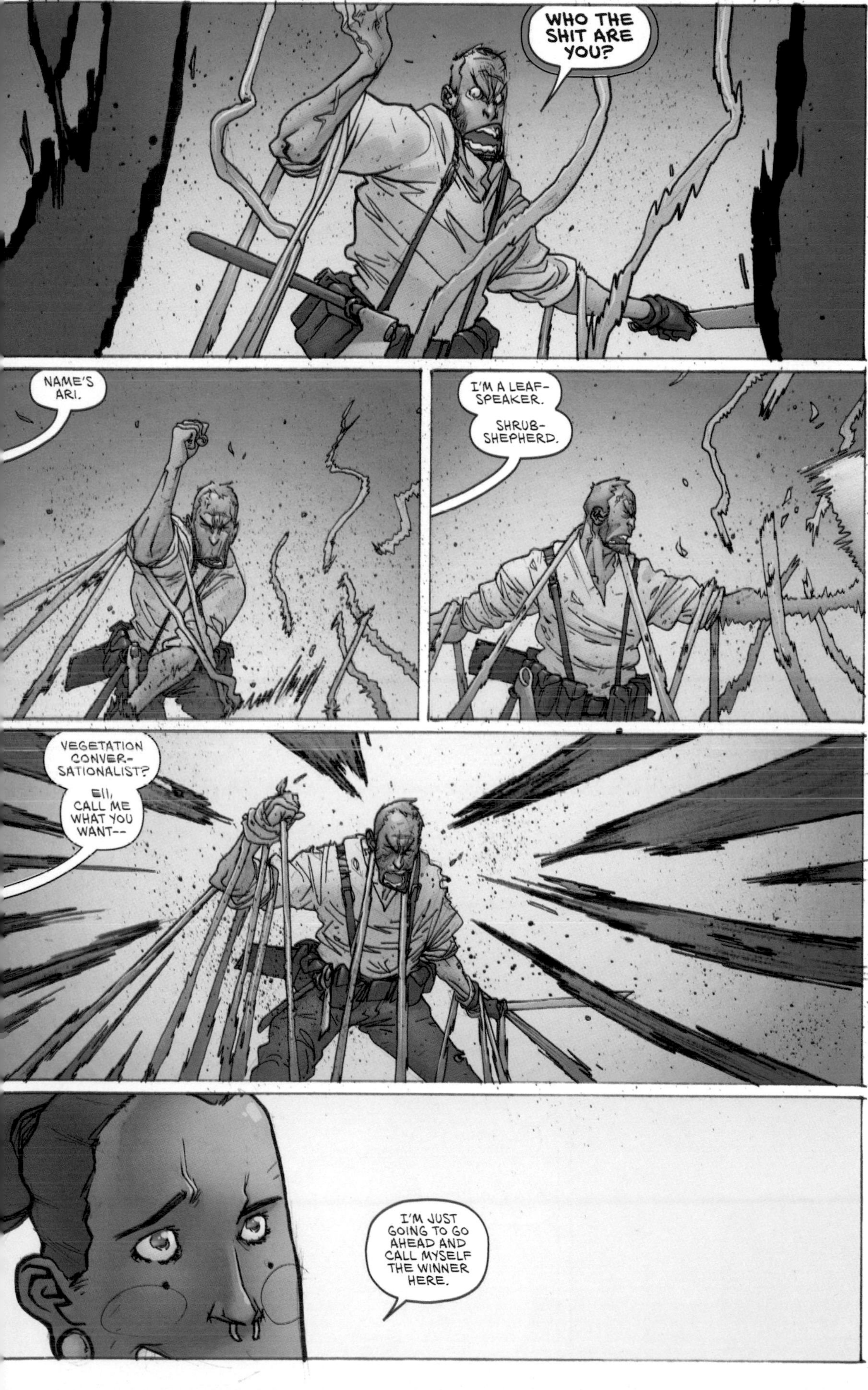
WHO THE SHIT ARE YOU?
NAME'S ARI.
I'M A LEAF-SPEAKER.
SHRUB-SHEPHERD.
VEGETATION CONVER-SATIONALIST?
EH, CALL ME WHAT YOU WANT--
I'M JUST GOING TO GO AHEAD AND CALL MYSELF THE WINNER HERE.

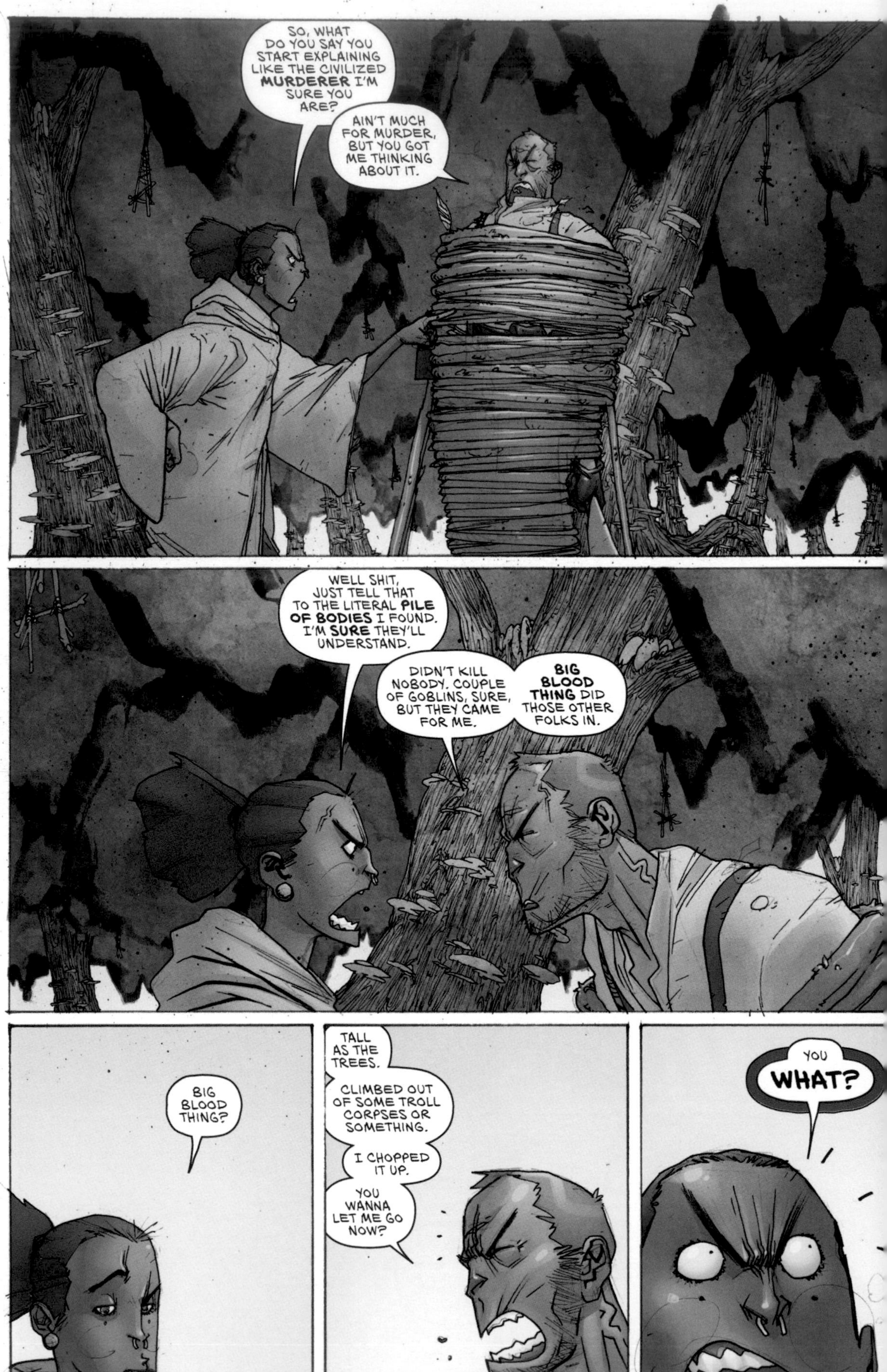

SO, WHAT DO YOU SAY YOU START EXPLAINING LIKE THE CIVILIZED **MURDERER** I'M SURE YOU ARE?
AIN'T MUCH FOR MURDER, BUT YOU GOT ME THINKING ABOUT IT.
WELL SHIT, JUST TELL THAT TO THE LITERAL **PILE OF BODIES** I FOUND. I'M **SURE** THEY'LL UNDERSTAND.
DIDN'T KILL NOBODY. COUPLE OF GOBLINS, SURE, BUT THEY CAME FOR ME.
BIG BLOOD THING DID THOSE OTHER FOLKS IN.
BIG BLOOD THING?
TALL AS THE TREES.
CLIMBED OUT OF SOME TROLL CORPSES OR SOMETHING.
I CHOPPED IT UP.
YOU WANNA LET ME GO NOW?
YOU **WHAT?**

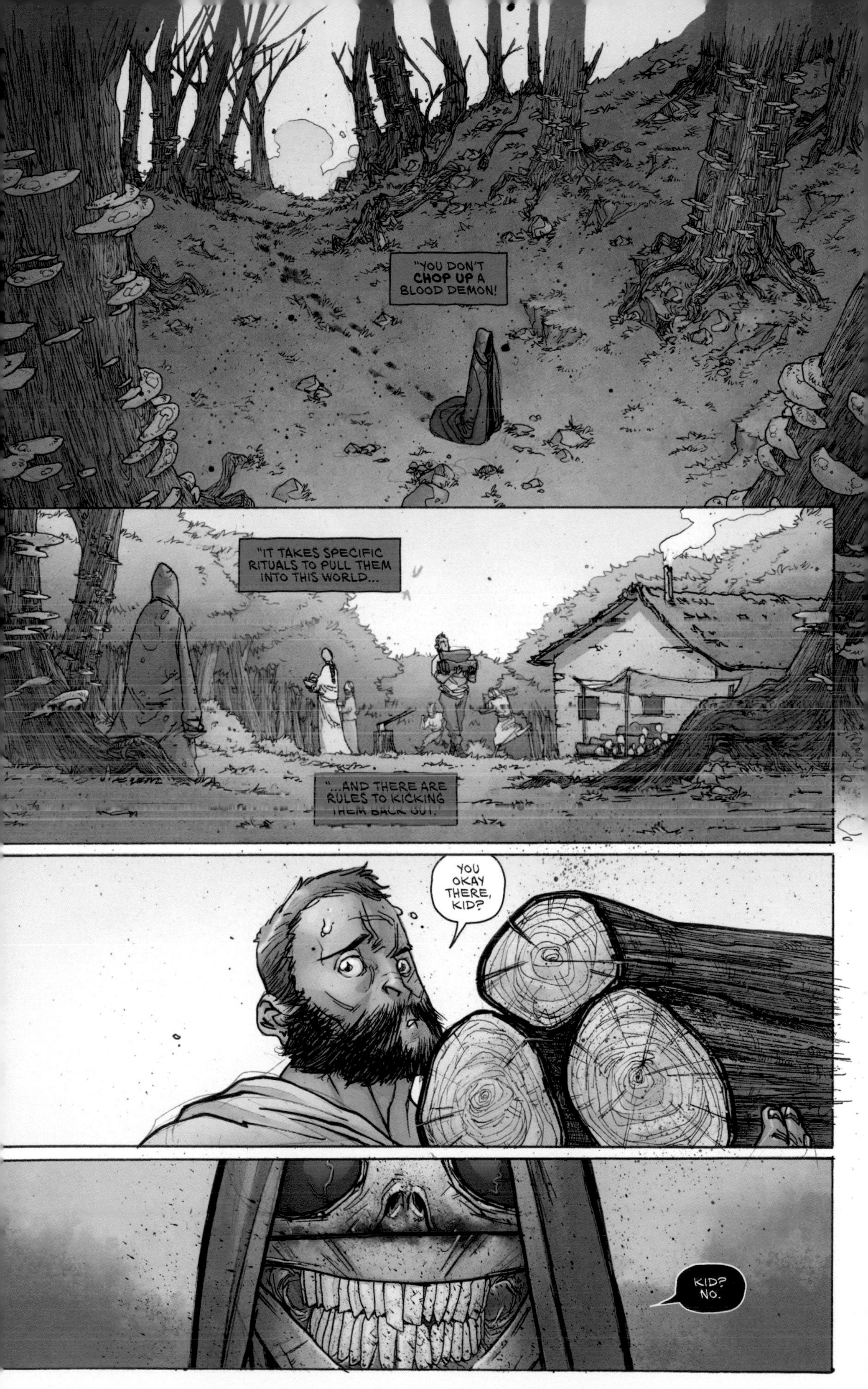
"YOU DON'T CHOP UP A BLOOD DEMON!
"IT TAKES SPECIFIC RITUALS TO PULL THEM INTO THIS WORLD...
"...AND THERE ARE RULES TO KICKING THEM BACK OUT.
YOU OKAY THERE, KID?
KID? NO.

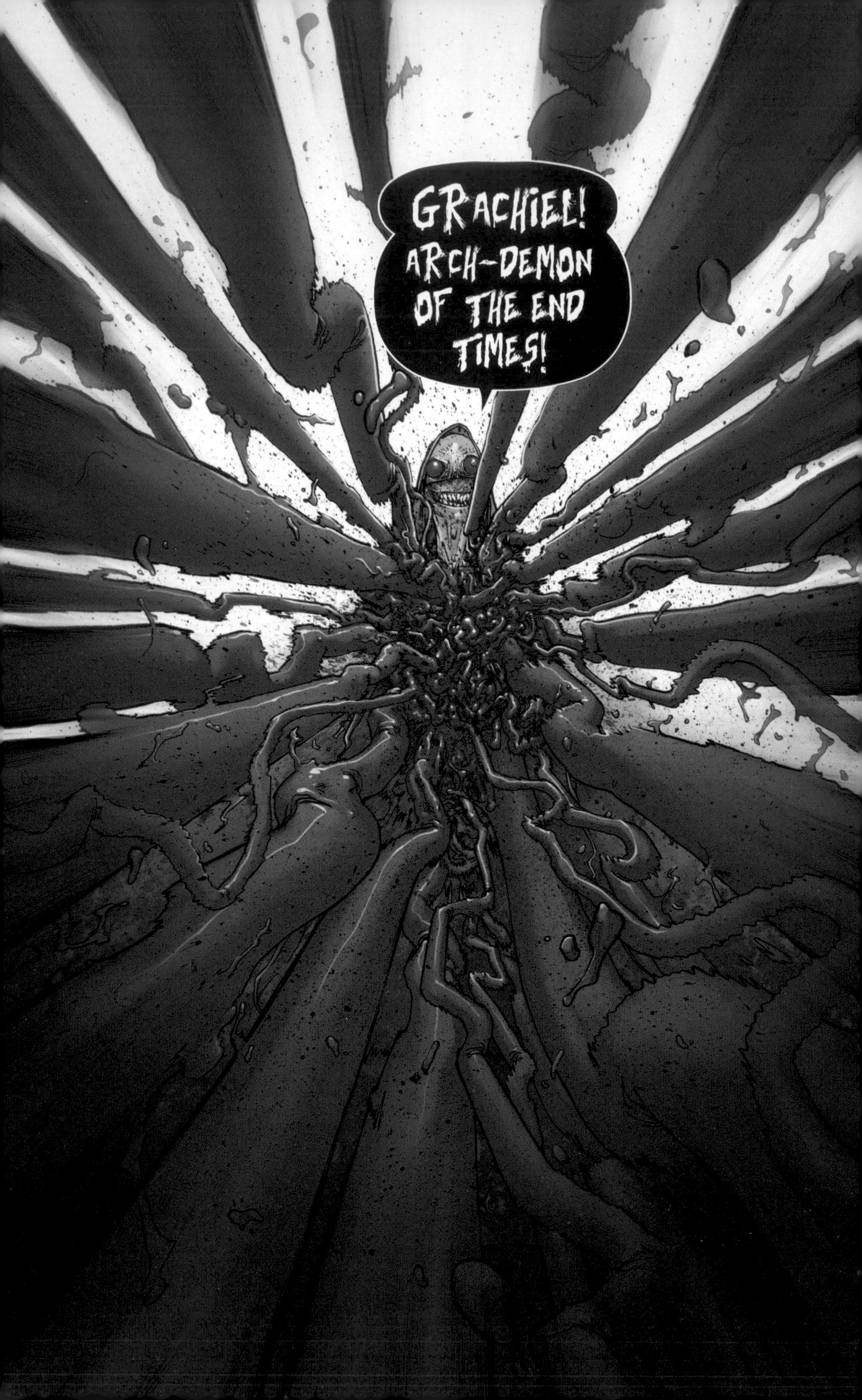
GRACHIEL! ARCH-DEMON OF THE END TIMES!

YOU GONNA LET ME DOWN NOW?

FINE.

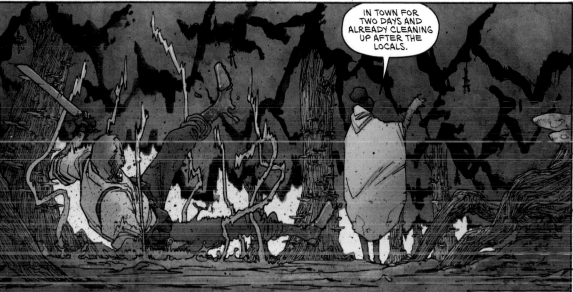

IN TOWN FOR TWO DAYS AND ALREADY CLEANING UP AFTER THE LOCALS.

UGH.

WHAT DO YOU THINK YOU'RE DOING?

WELL...

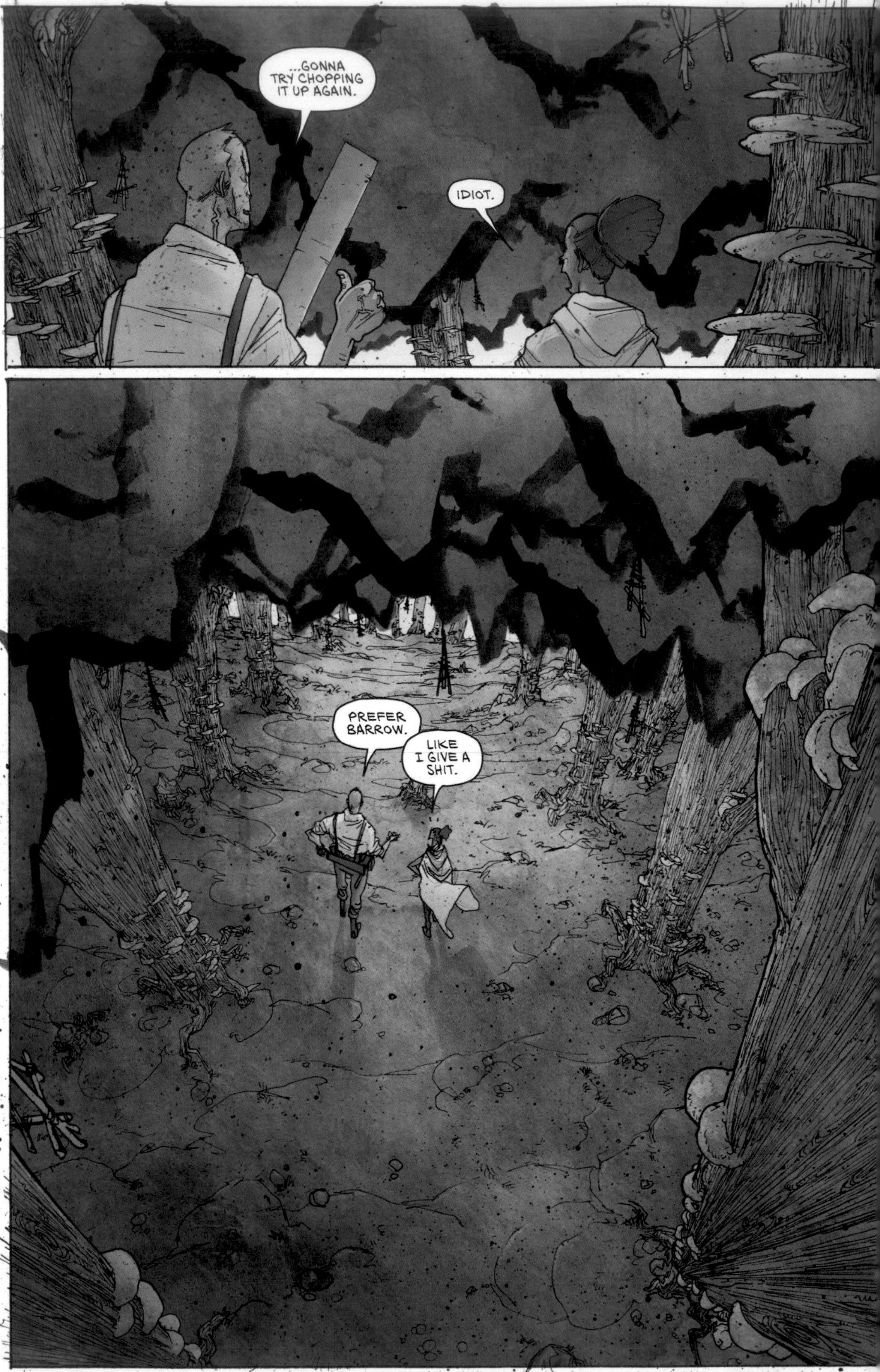
...GONNA TRY CHOPPING IT UP AGAIN.
IDIOT.
PREFER BARROW.
LIKE I GIVE A SHIT.

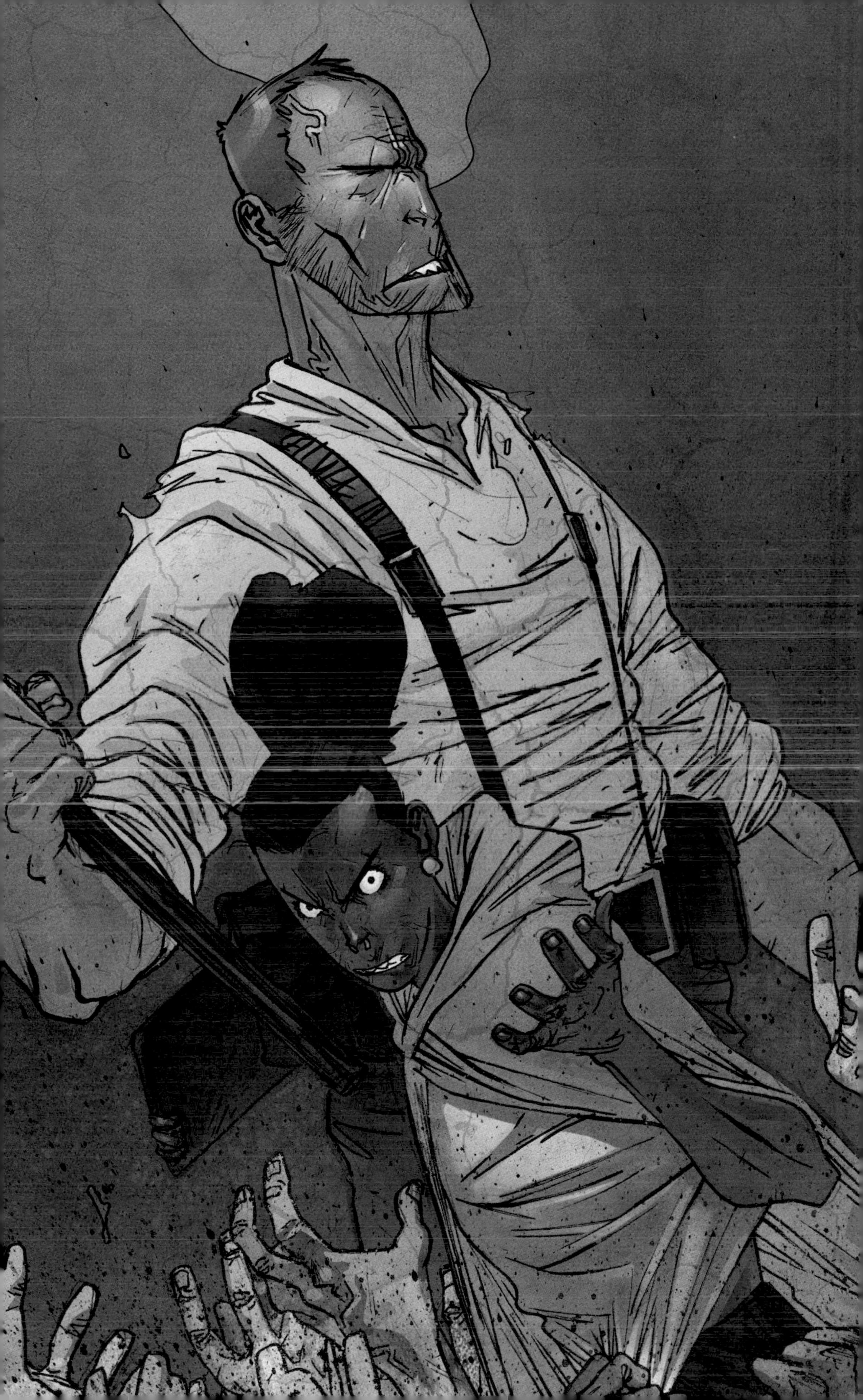

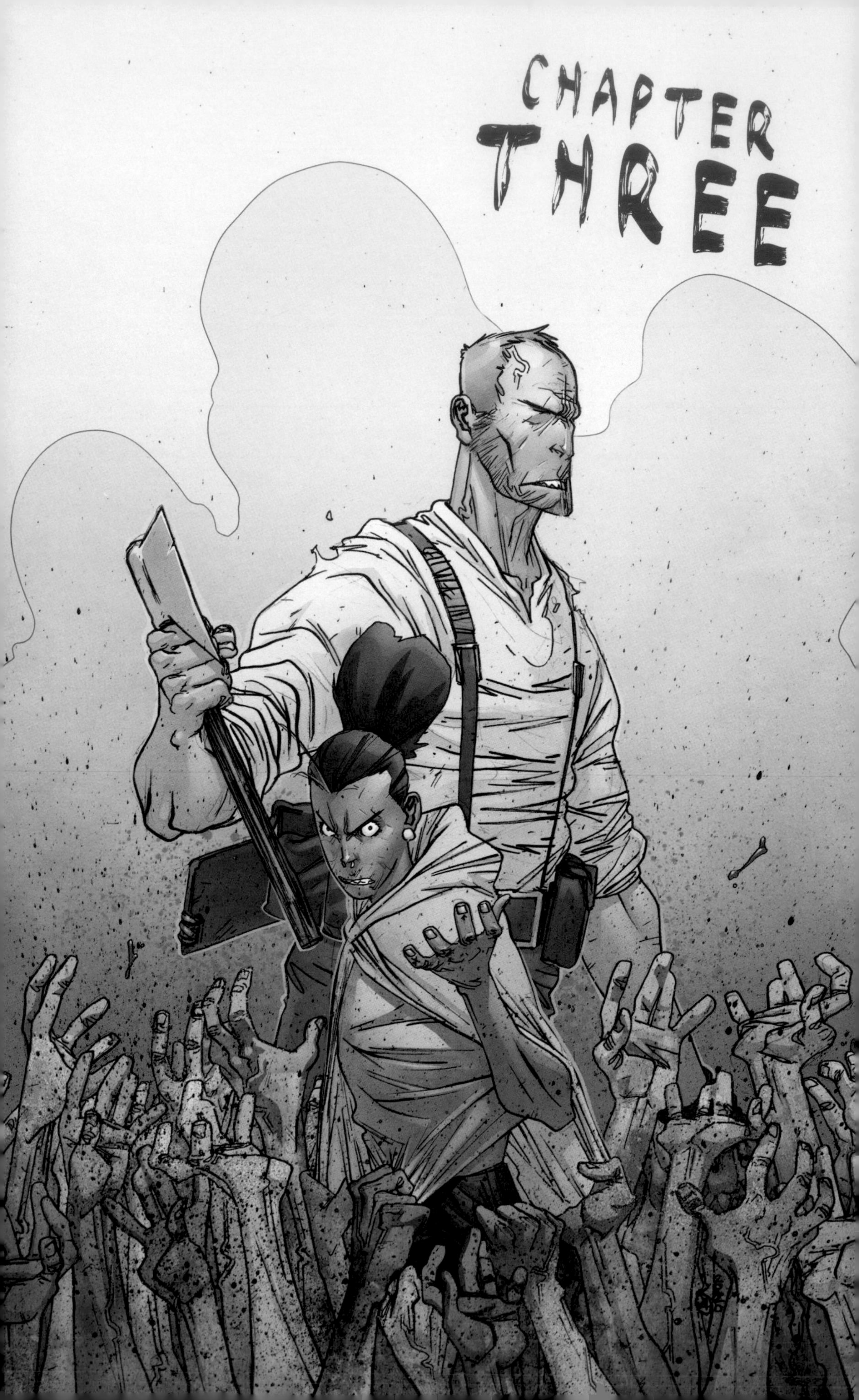
CHAPTER
THREE

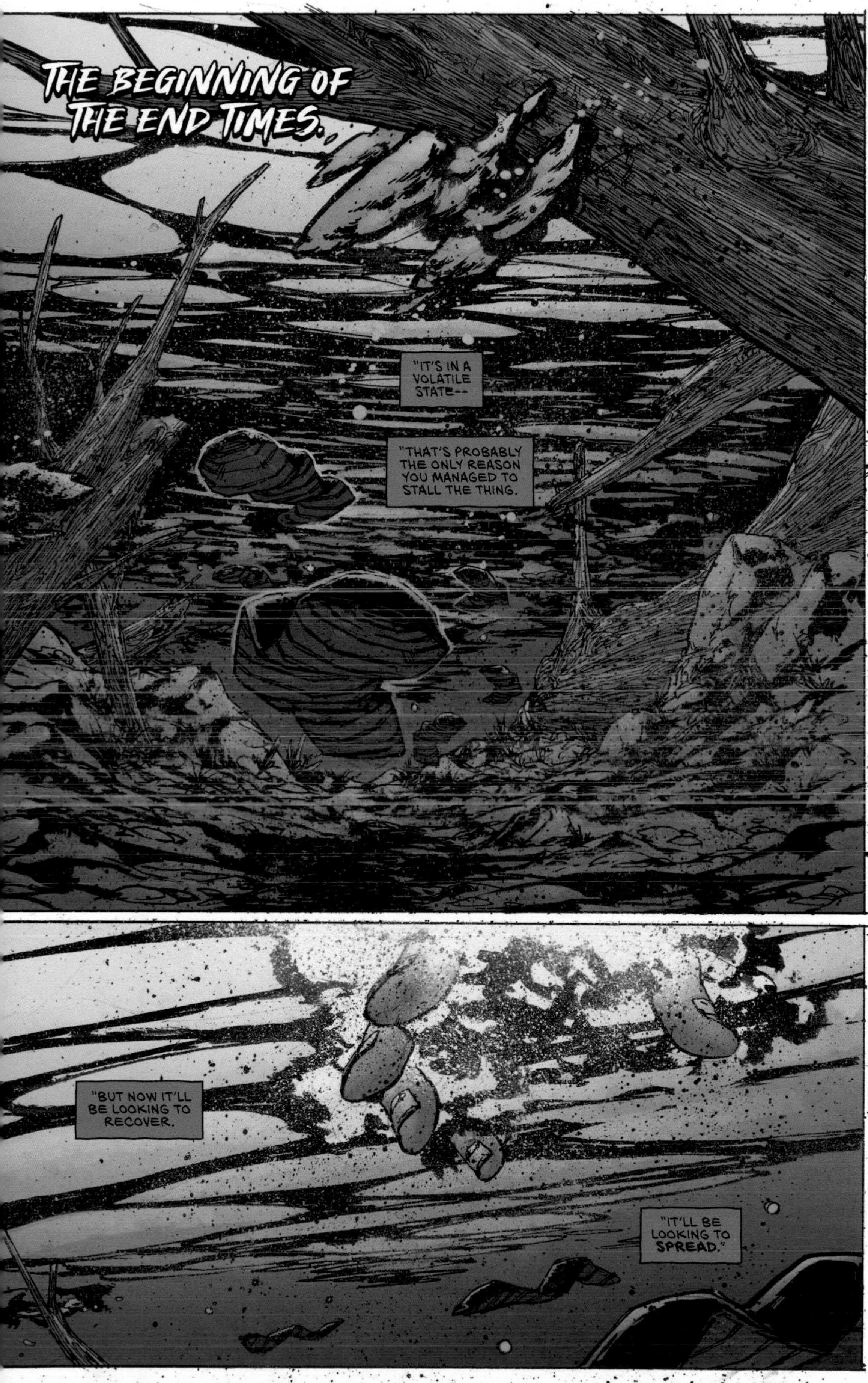
THE BEGINNING OF THE END TIMES.
"IT'S IN A VOLATILE STATE--
"THAT'S PROBABLY THE ONLY REASON YOU MANAGED TO STALL THE THING.
"BUT NOW IT'LL BE LOOKING TO RECOVER.
"IT'LL BE LOOKING TO SPREAD."

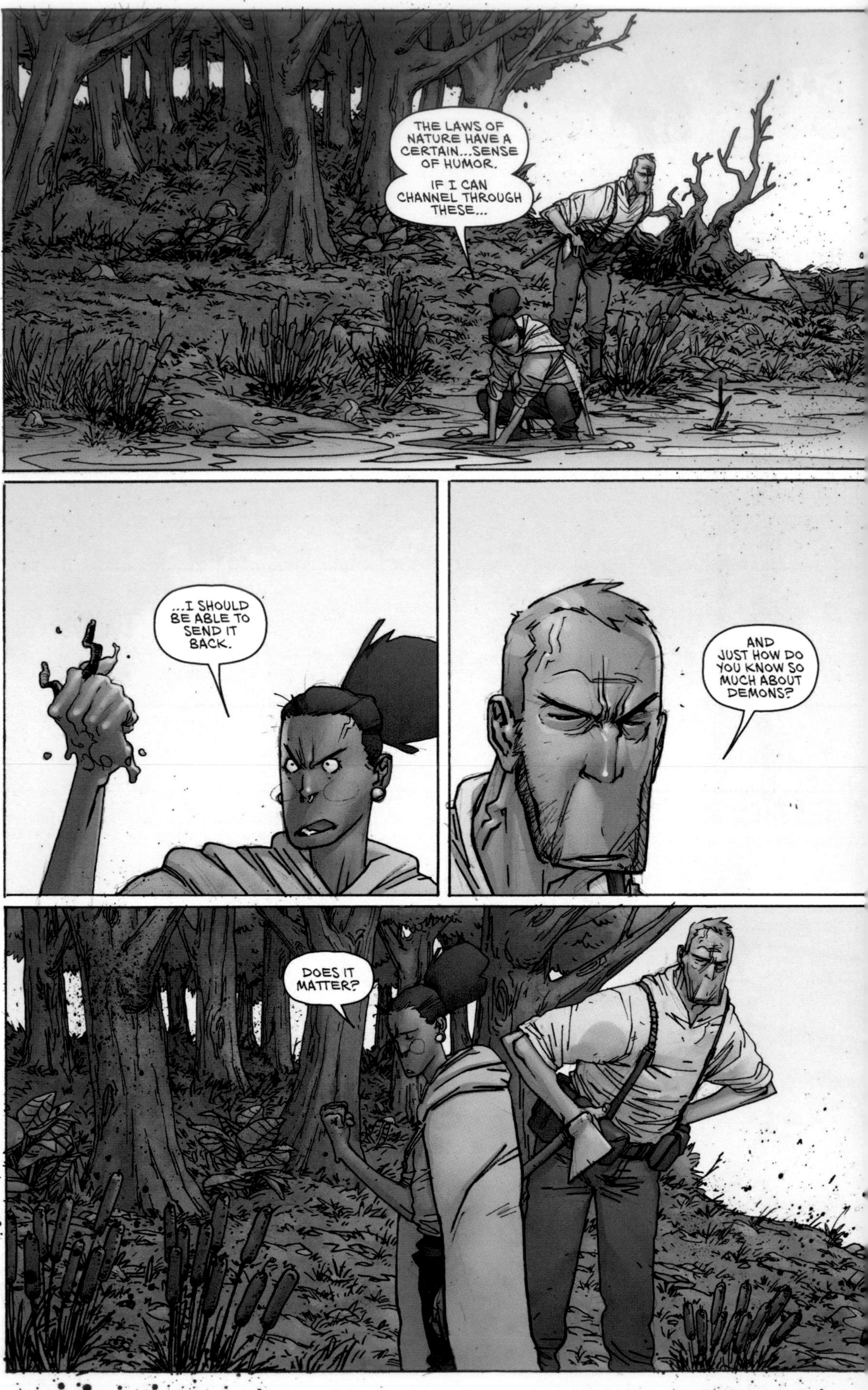
THE LAWS OF NATURE HAVE A CERTAIN...SENSE OF HUMOR.
IF I CAN CHANNEL THROUGH THESE...
...I SHOULD BE ABLE TO SEND IT BACK.
AND JUST HOW DO YOU KNOW SO MUCH ABOUT DEMONS?
DOES IT MATTER?

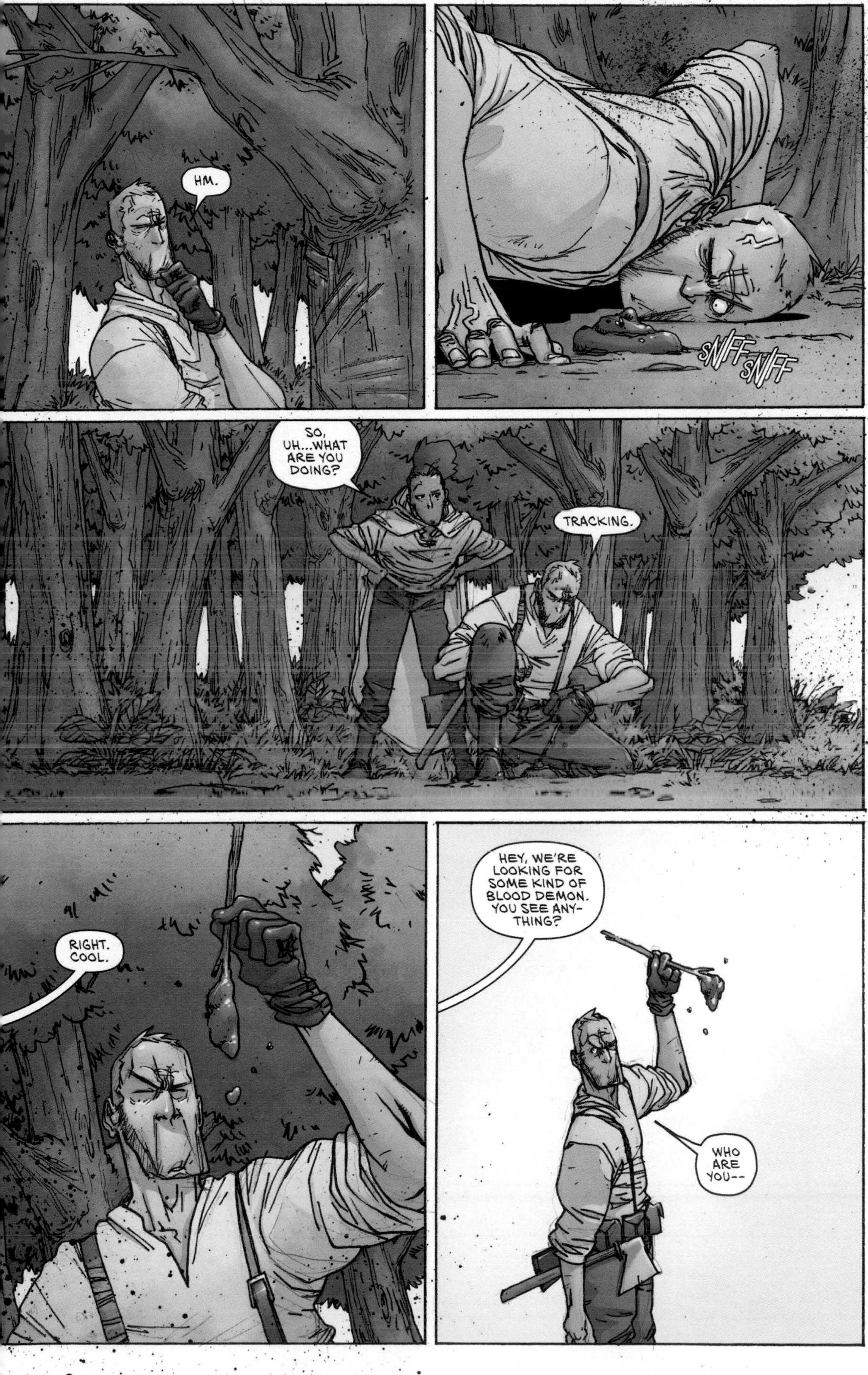
HM.
SNIFF SNIFF
SO, UH...WHAT ARE YOU DOING?
TRACKING.
RIGHT. COOL.
HEY, WE'RE LOOKING FOR SOME KIND OF BLOOD DEMON. YOU SEE ANY-THING?
WHO ARE YOU--

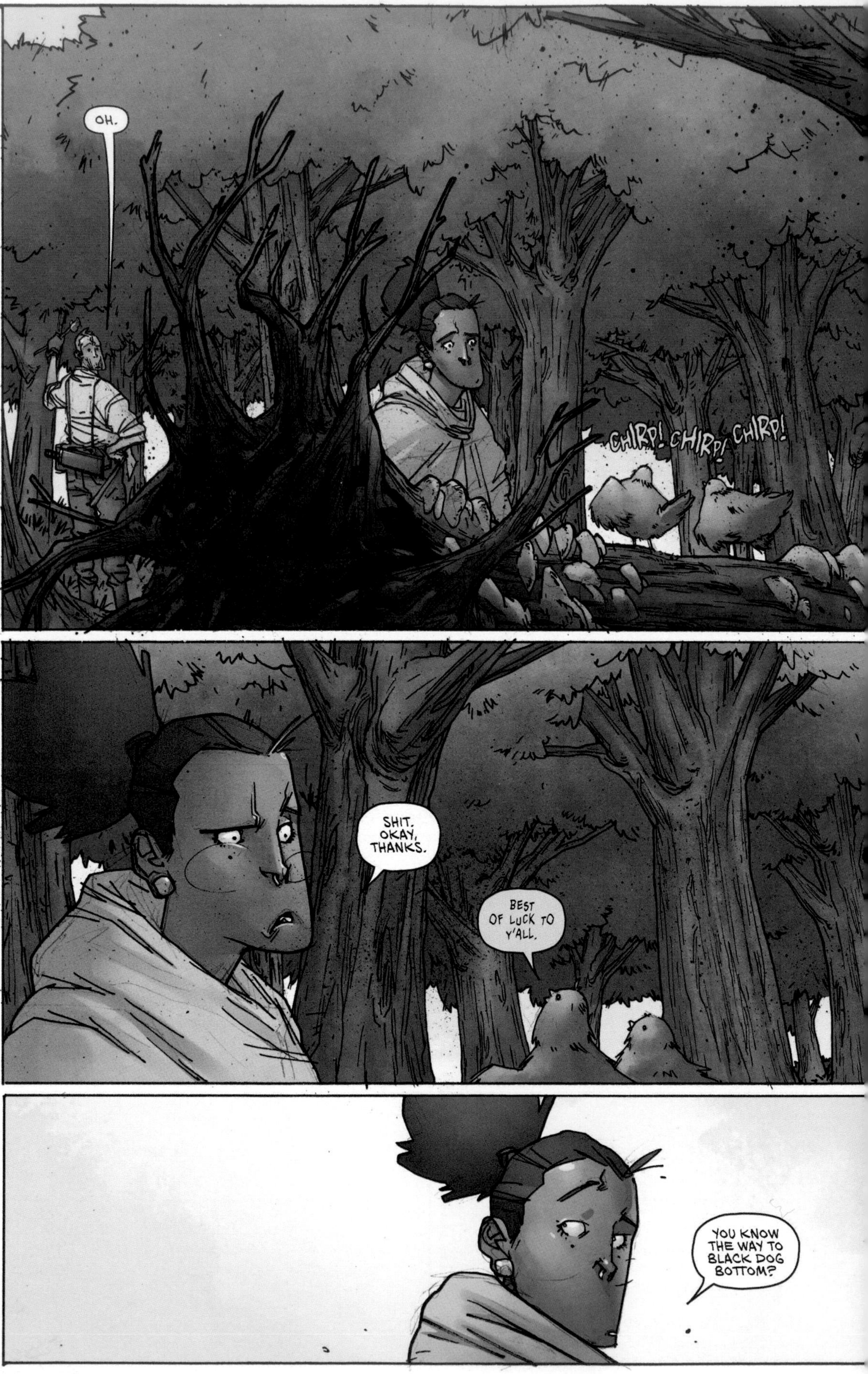
OH.
CHIRP! CHIRP! CHIRP!
SHIT. OKAY, THANKS.
BEST OF LUCK TO Y'ALL.
YOU KNOW THE WAY TO BLACK DOG BOTTOM?

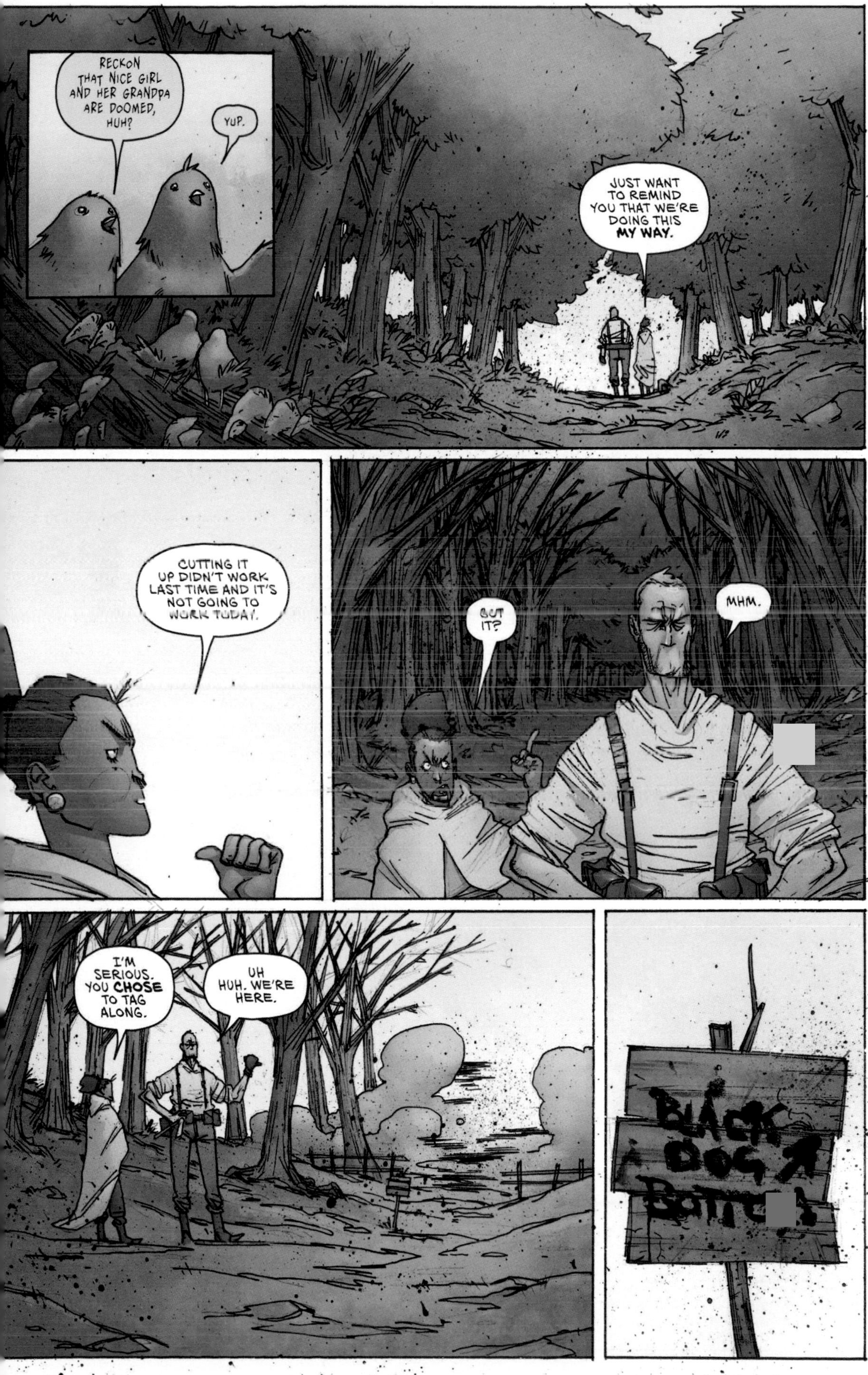
RECKON THAT NICE GIRL AND HER GRANDPA ARE DOOMED, HUH?
YUP.
JUST WANT TO REMIND YOU THAT WE'RE DOING THIS **MY WAY.**
CUTTING IT UP DIDN'T WORK LAST TIME AND IT'S NOT GOING TO WORK TODAY.
BUT IT?
MHM.
I'M SERIOUS. YOU **CHOSE** TO TAG ALONG.
UH HUH. WE'RE HERE.
BLACK DOG

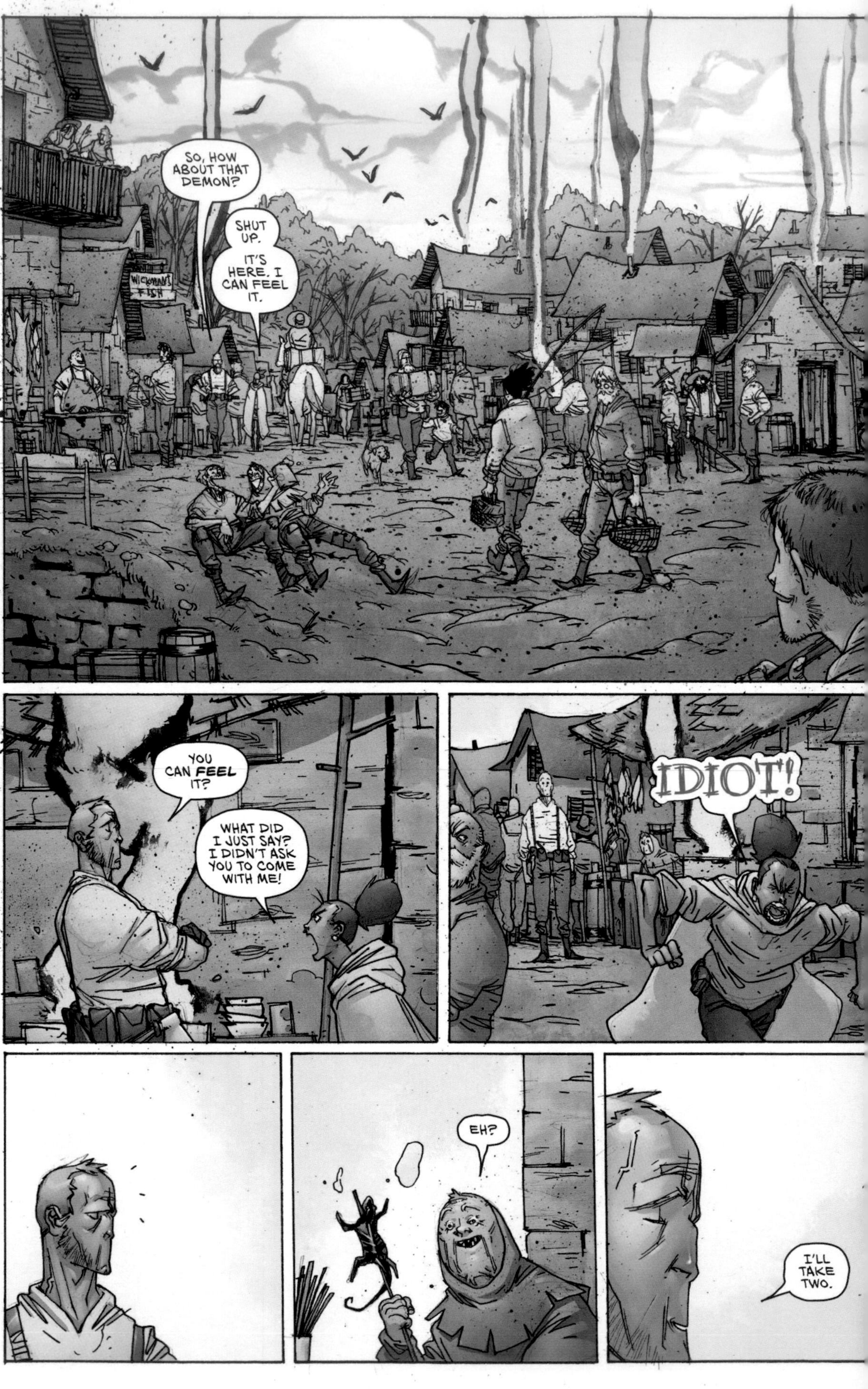

WICKMAN'S FISH
SO, HOW ABOUT THAT DEMON?
SHUT UP.
IT'S HERE. I CAN FEEL IT.
YOU CAN FEEL IT?
WHAT DID I JUST SAY? I DIDN'T ASK YOU TO COME WITH ME!
IDIOT!
EH?
I'LL TAKE TWO.

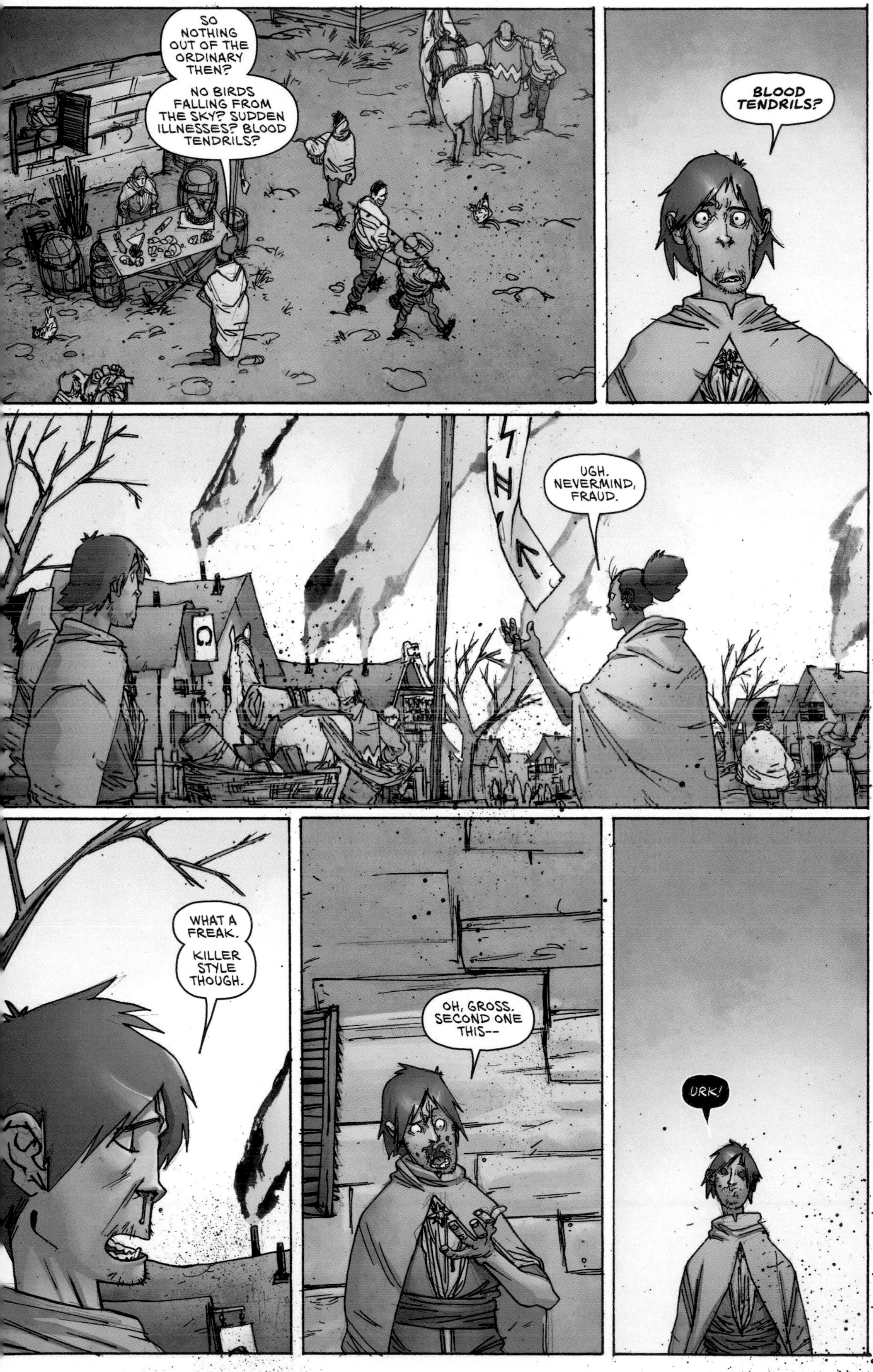
SO NOTHING OUT OF THE ORDINARY THEN?
NO BIRDS FALLING FROM THE SKY? SUDDEN ILLNESSES? BLOOD TENDRILS?
BLOOD TENDRILS?
UGH. NEVERMIND, FRAUD.
WHAT A FREAK.
KILLER STYLE THOUGH.
OH, GROSS. SECOND ONE THIS--
URK!

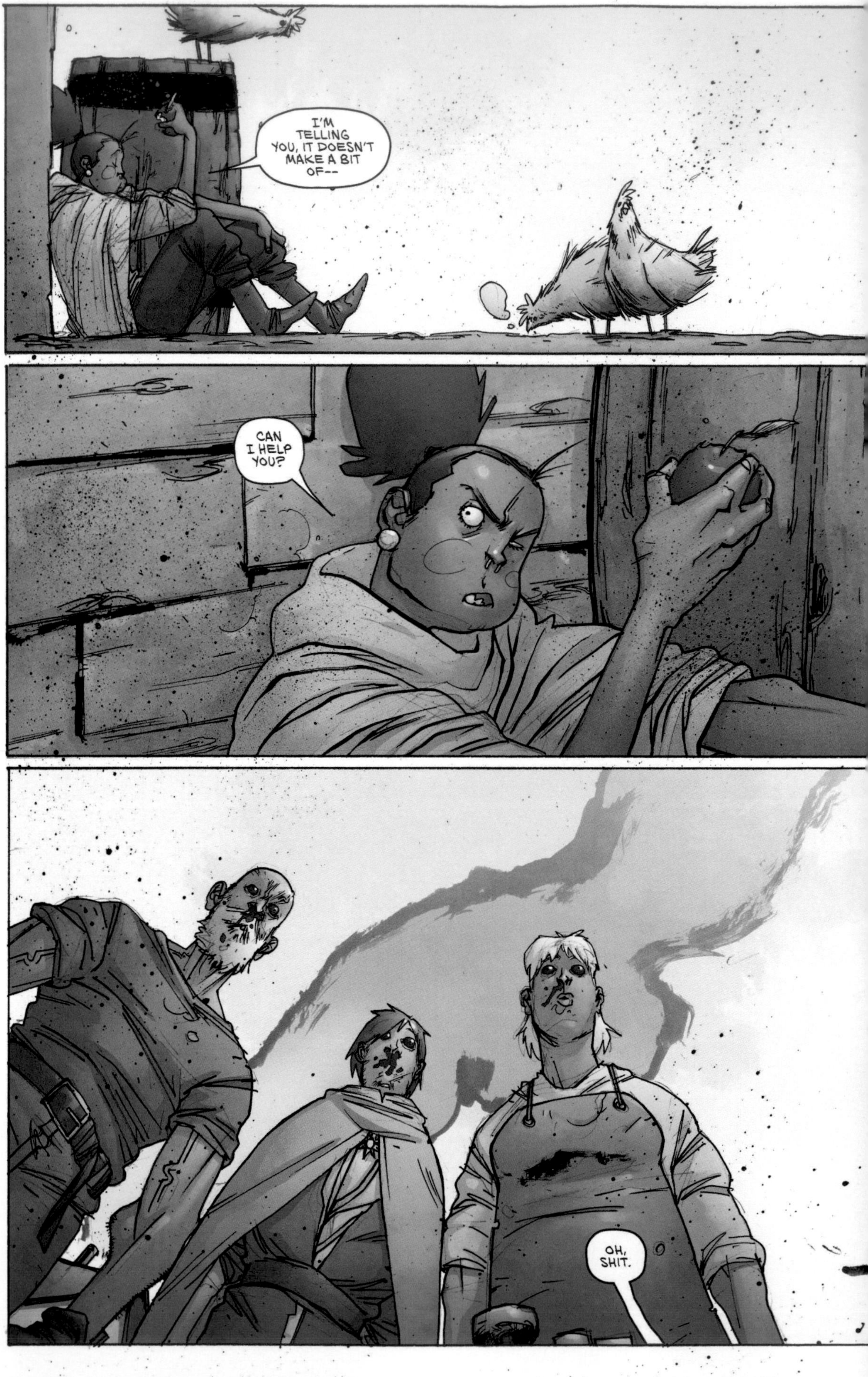
I'M TELLING YOU, IT DOESN'T MAKE A BIT OF--
CAN I HELP YOU?
OH, SHIT.

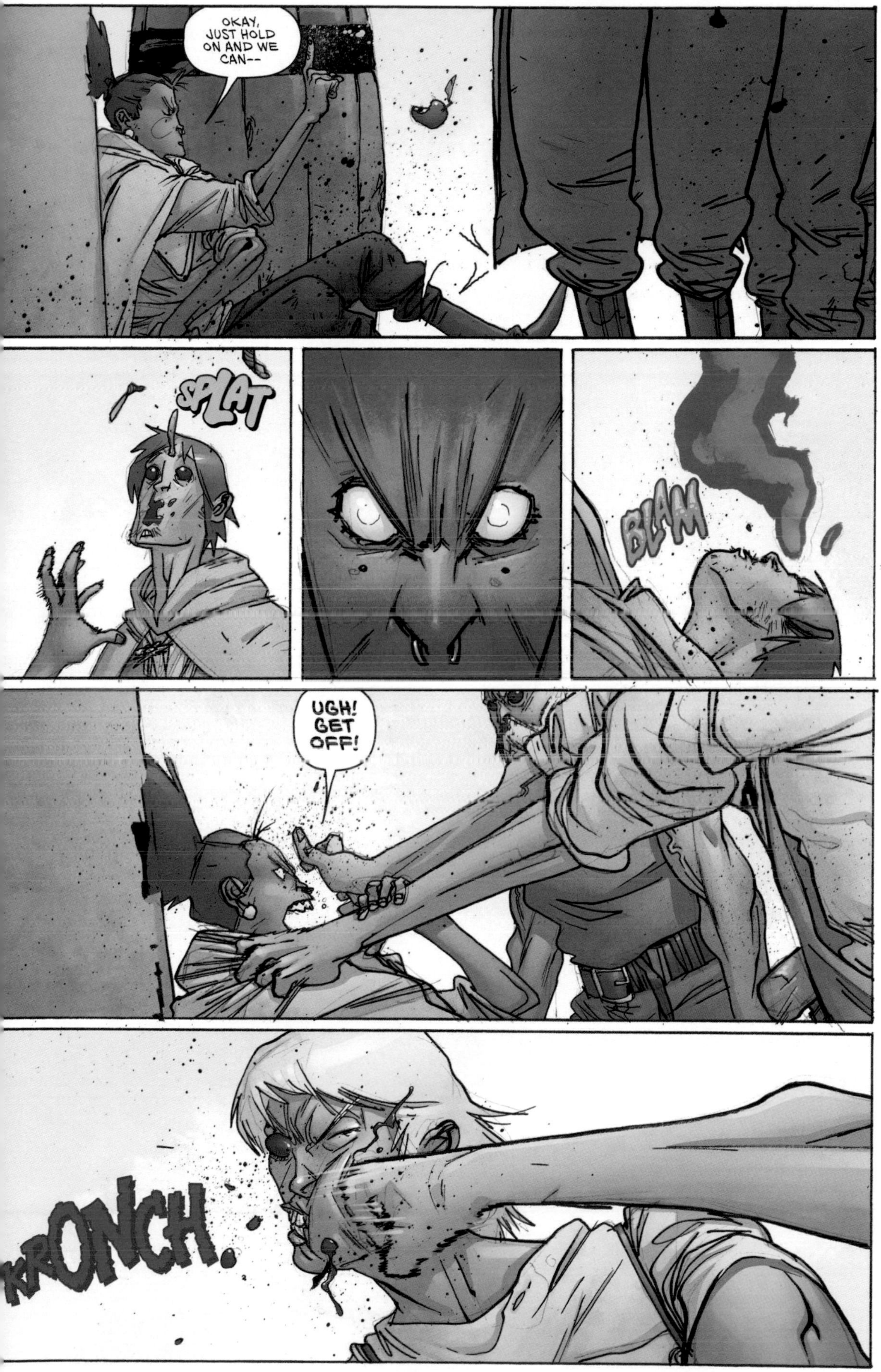
OKAY, JUST HOLD ON AND WE CAN--
SPLAT
BLAM
UGH! GET OFF!
KRONCH.

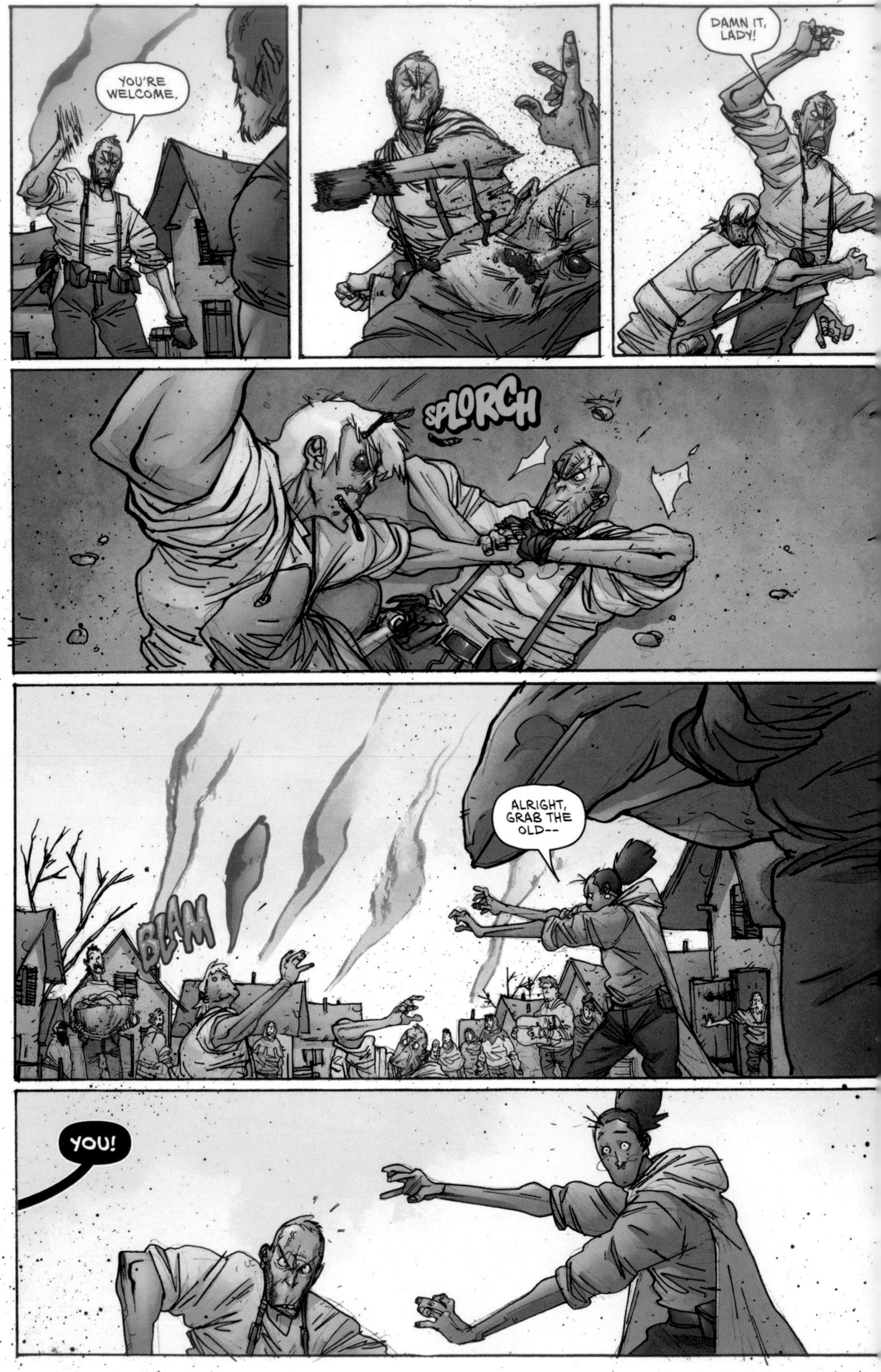
YOU'RE WELCOME.
DAMN IT, LADY!
SPLORCH
ALRIGHT, GRAB THE OLD--
BLAM
YOU!

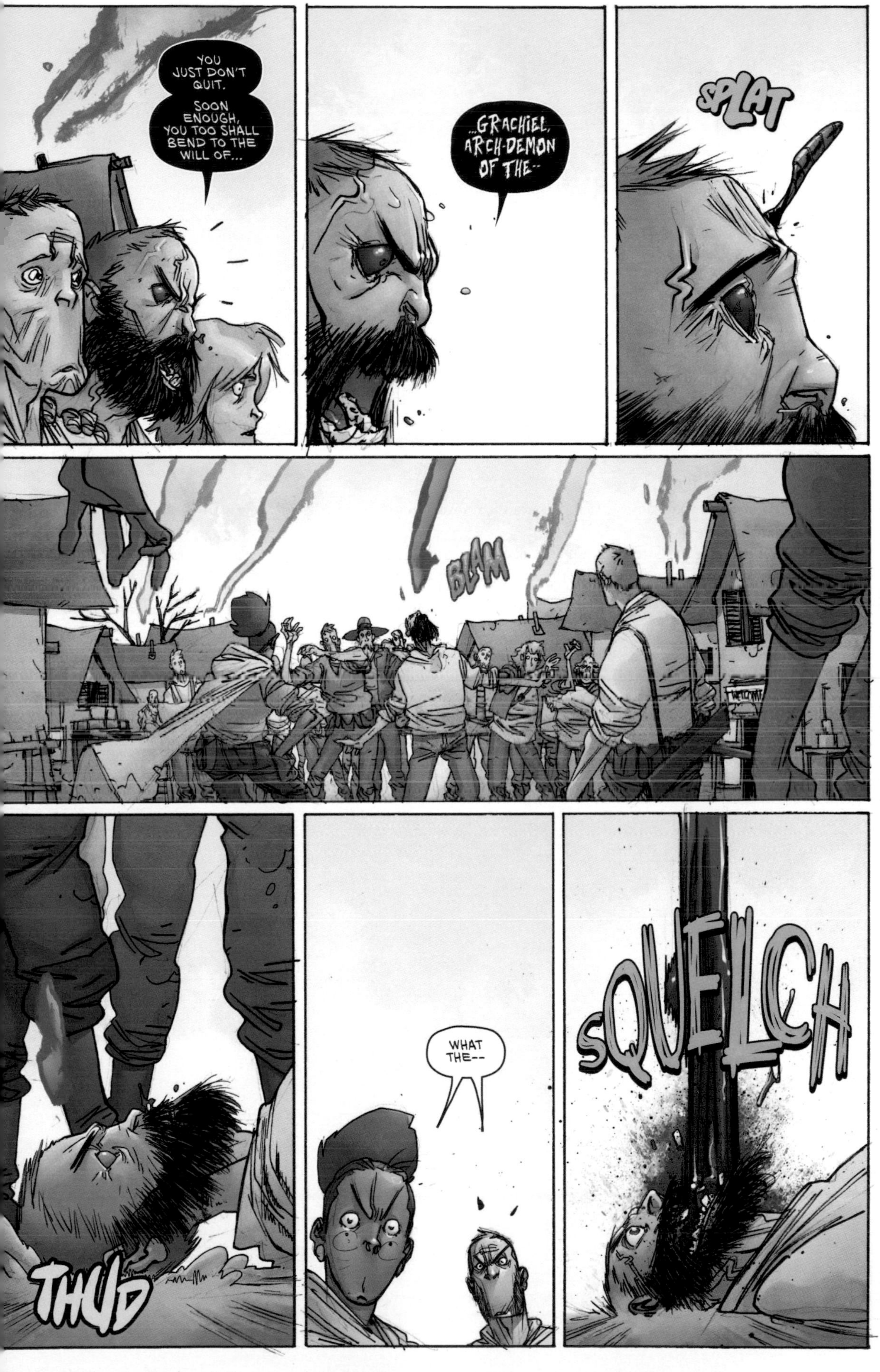
YOU JUST DON'T QUIT.
SOON ENOUGH, YOU TOO SHALL BEND TO THE WILL OF...
...GRACHIEL, ARCH-DEMON OF THE--
SPLAT
BLAM
THUD
WHAT THE--
SQUELCH

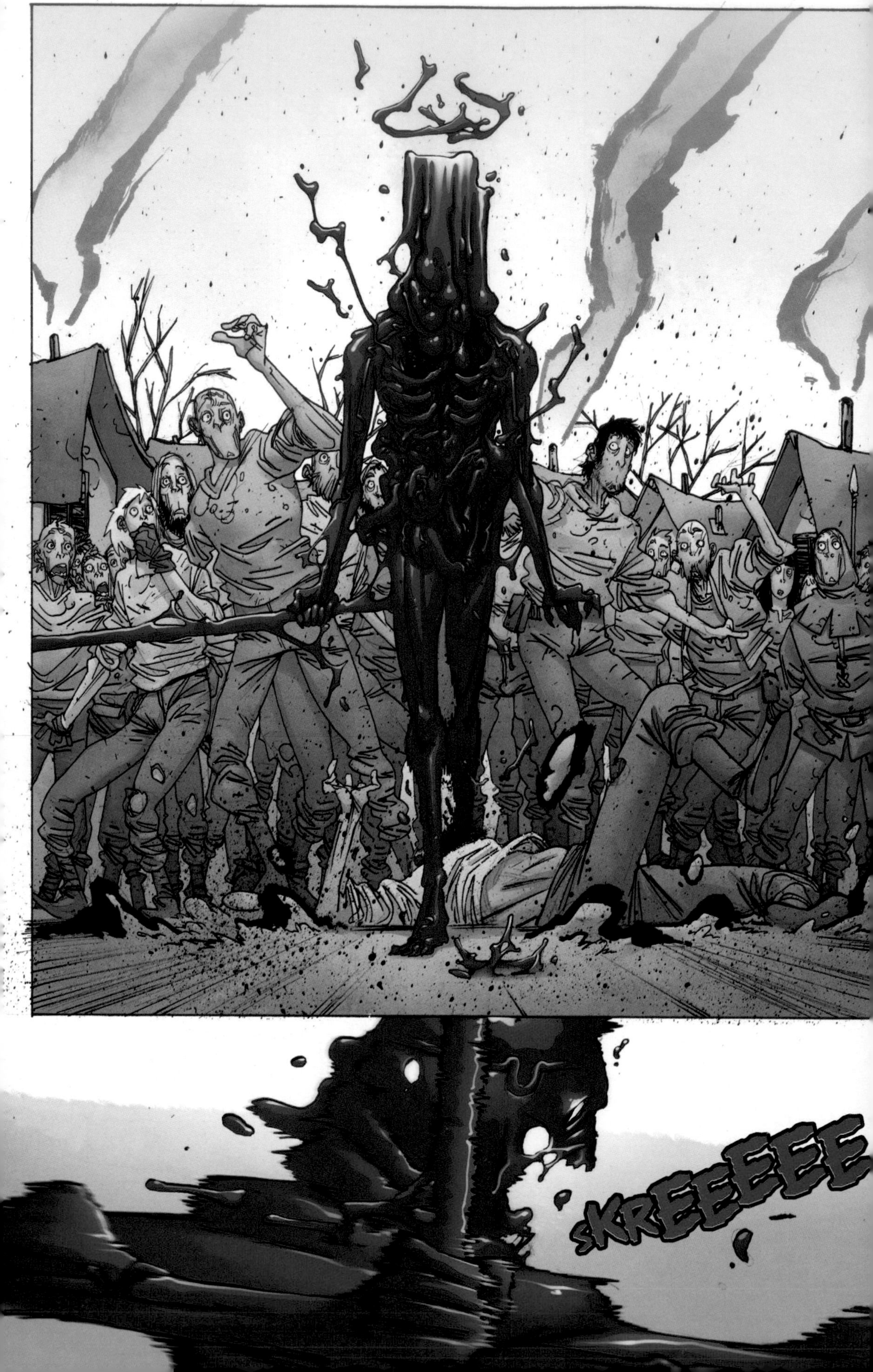
sKREEEEEE

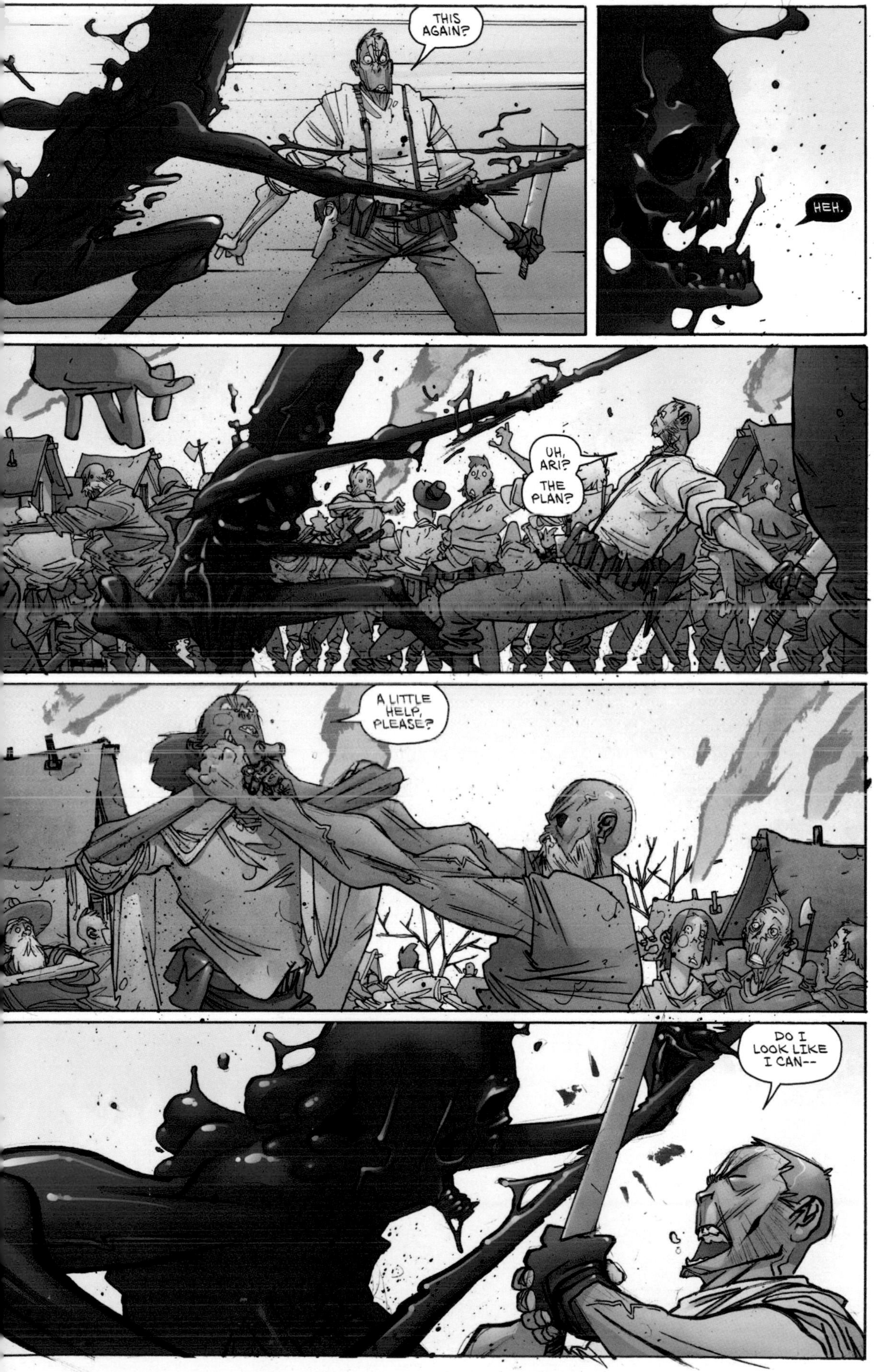
THIS AGAIN?
HEH.
UH, ARI?
THE PLAN?
A LITTLE HELP, PLEASE?
DO I LOOK LIKE I CAN--

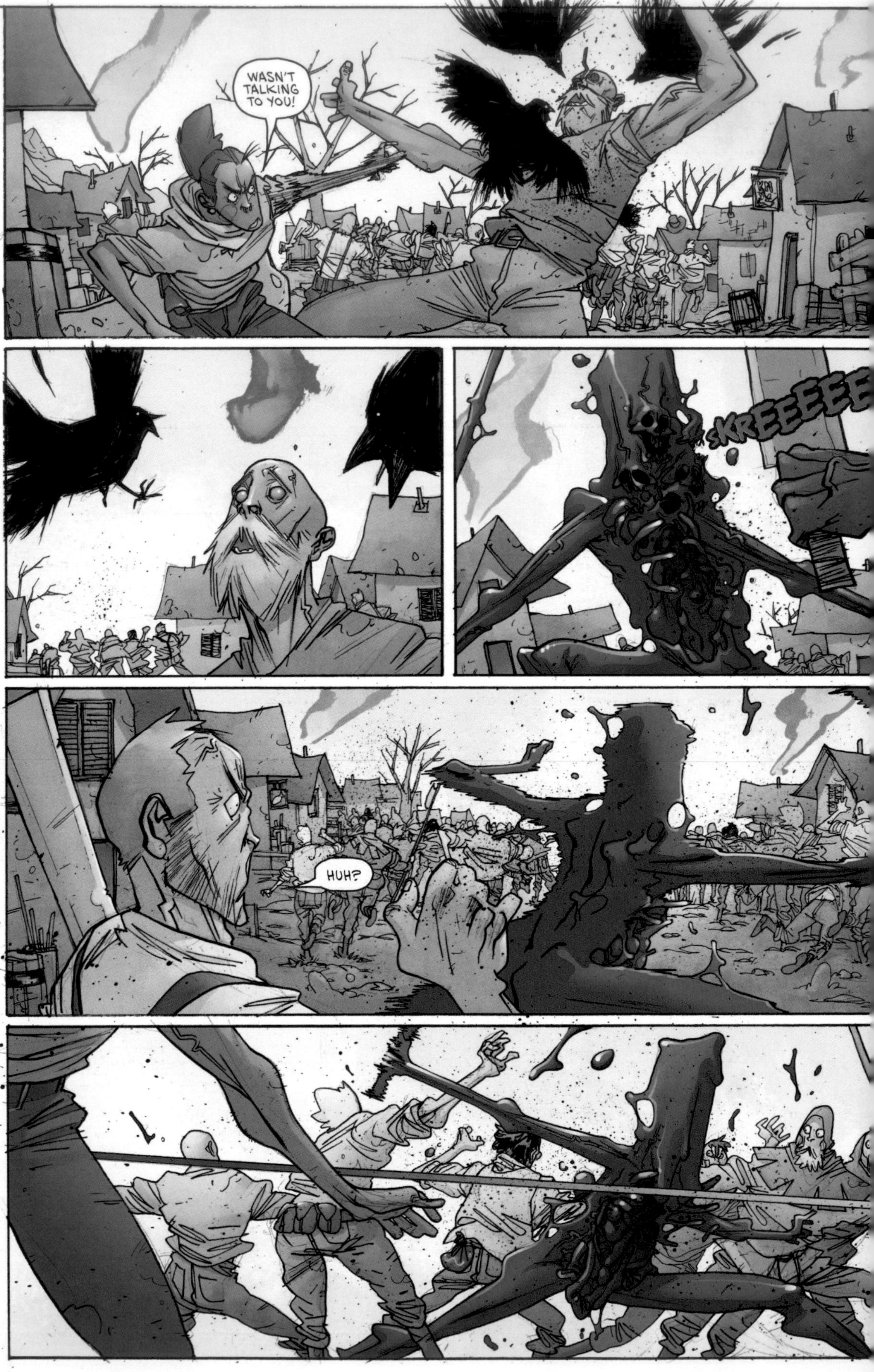
WASN'T TALKING TO YOU!
SKREEEEEE
HUH?

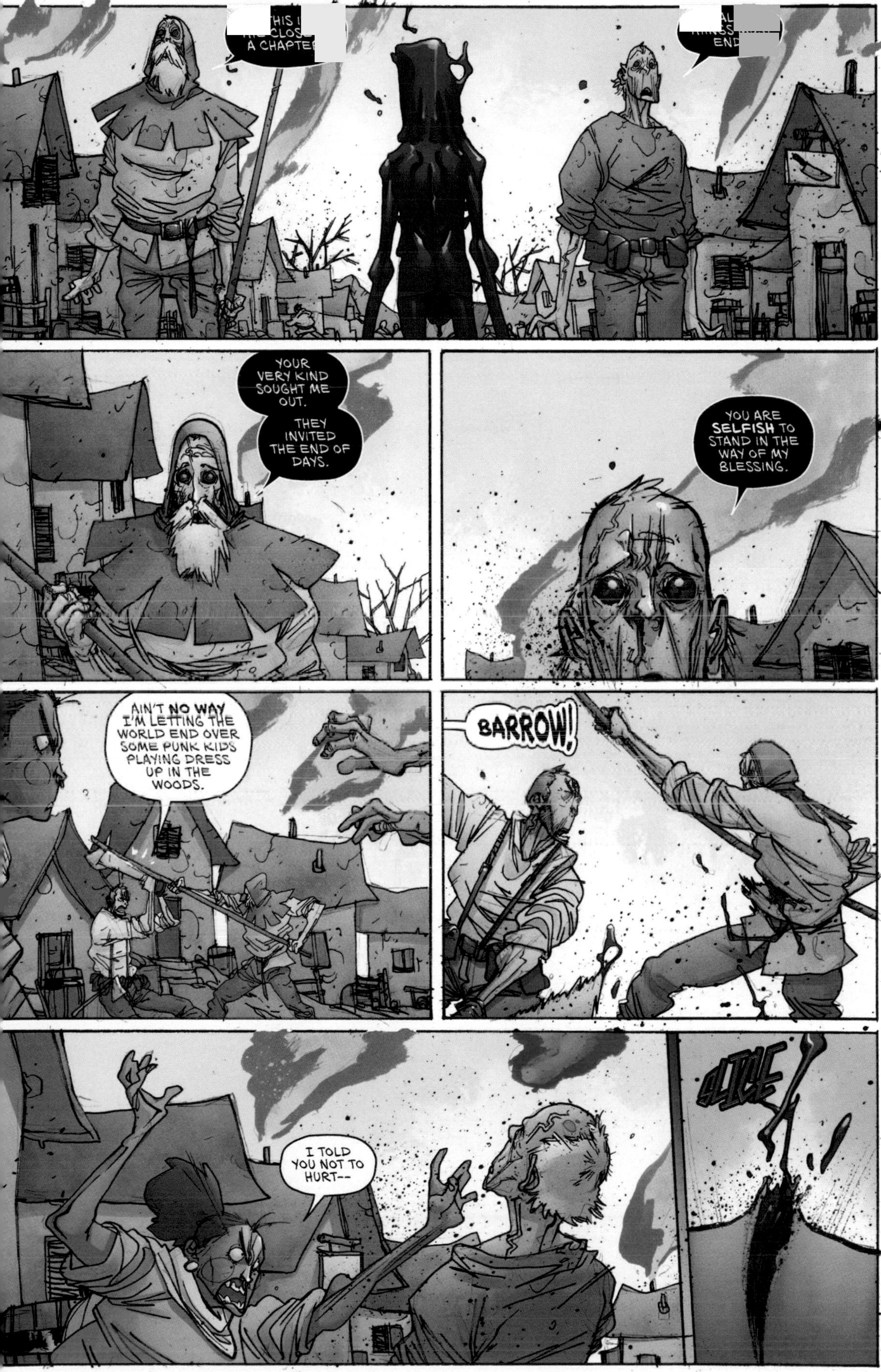
YOUR VERY KIND SOUGHT ME OUT.
THEY INVITED THE END OF DAYS.
YOU ARE SELFISH TO STAND IN THE WAY OF MY BLESSING.
AIN'T NO WAY I'M LETTING THE WORLD END OVER SOME PUNK KIDS PLAYING DRESS UP IN THE WOODS.
BARROW!
I TOLD YOU NOT TO HURT--
SLICE

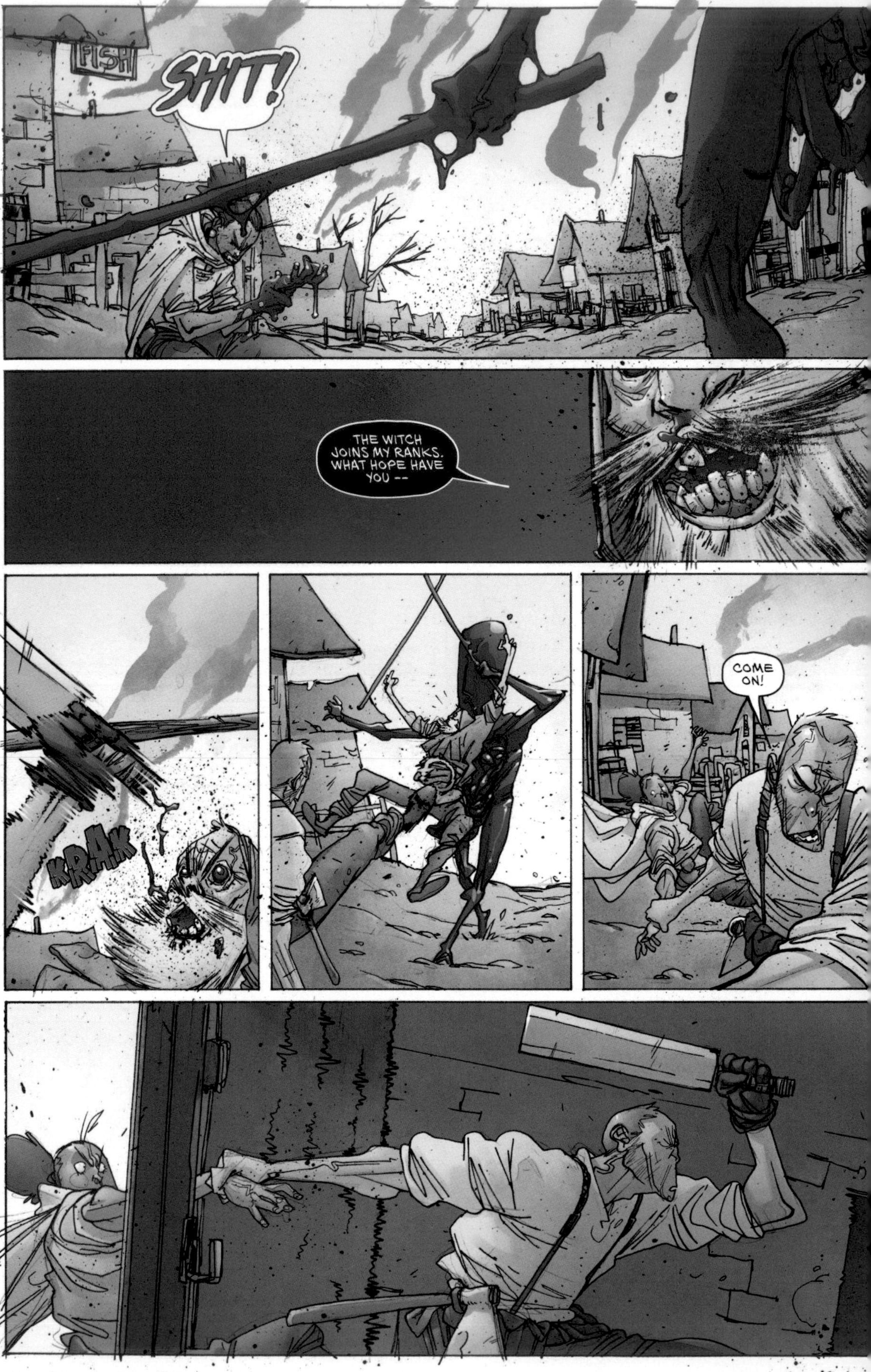
FISH
SHIT!
THE WITCH JOINS MY RANKS. WHAT HOPE HAVE YOU --
KRAK
COME ON!

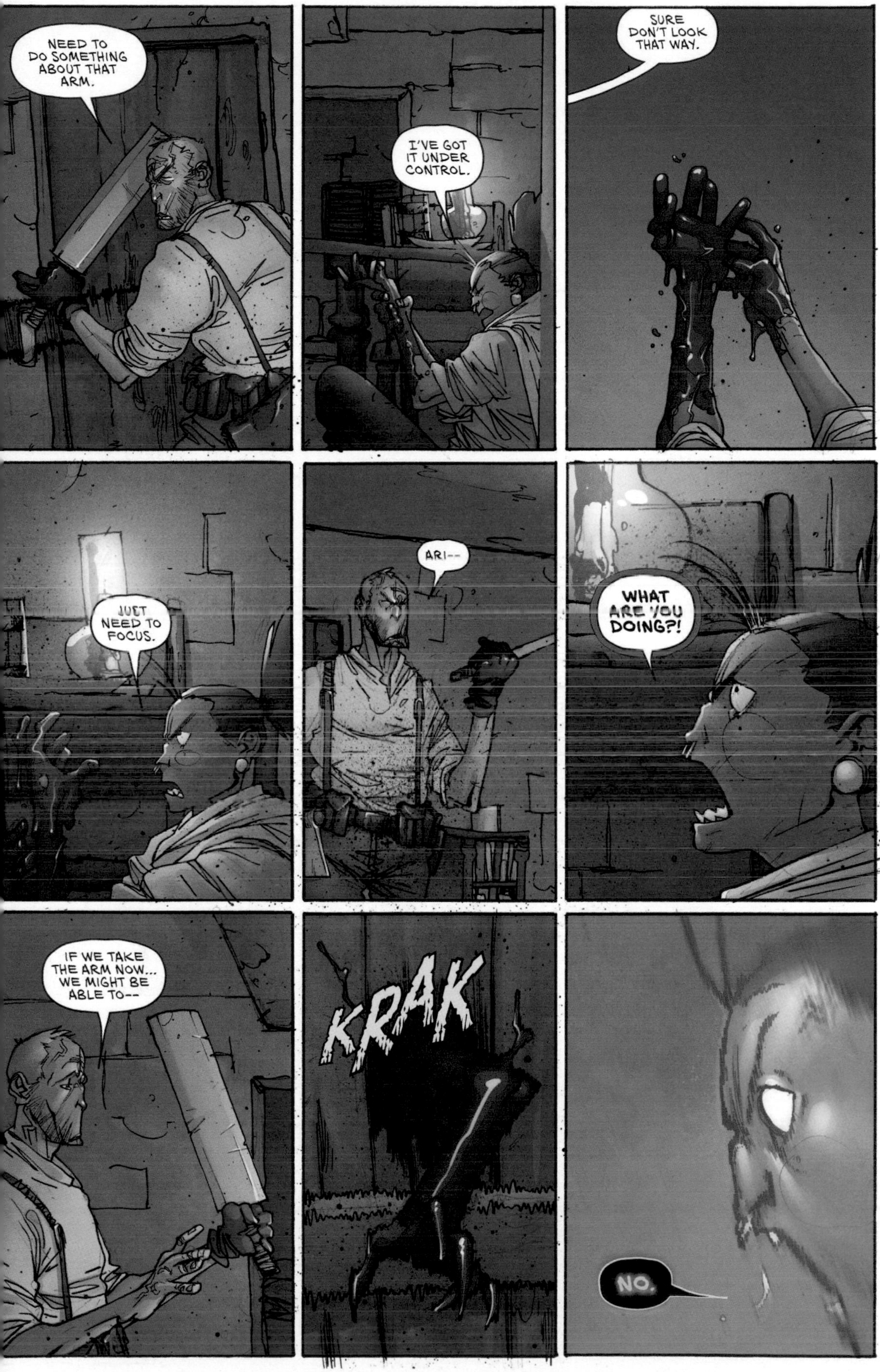
NEED TO DO SOMETHING ABOUT THAT ARM.
I'VE GOT IT UNDER CONTROL.
SURE DON'T LOOK THAT WAY.
JUST NEED TO FOCUS.
ARI--
WHAT ARE YOU DOING?!
IF WE TAKE THE ARM NOW... WE MIGHT BE ABLE TO--
KRAK
NO.

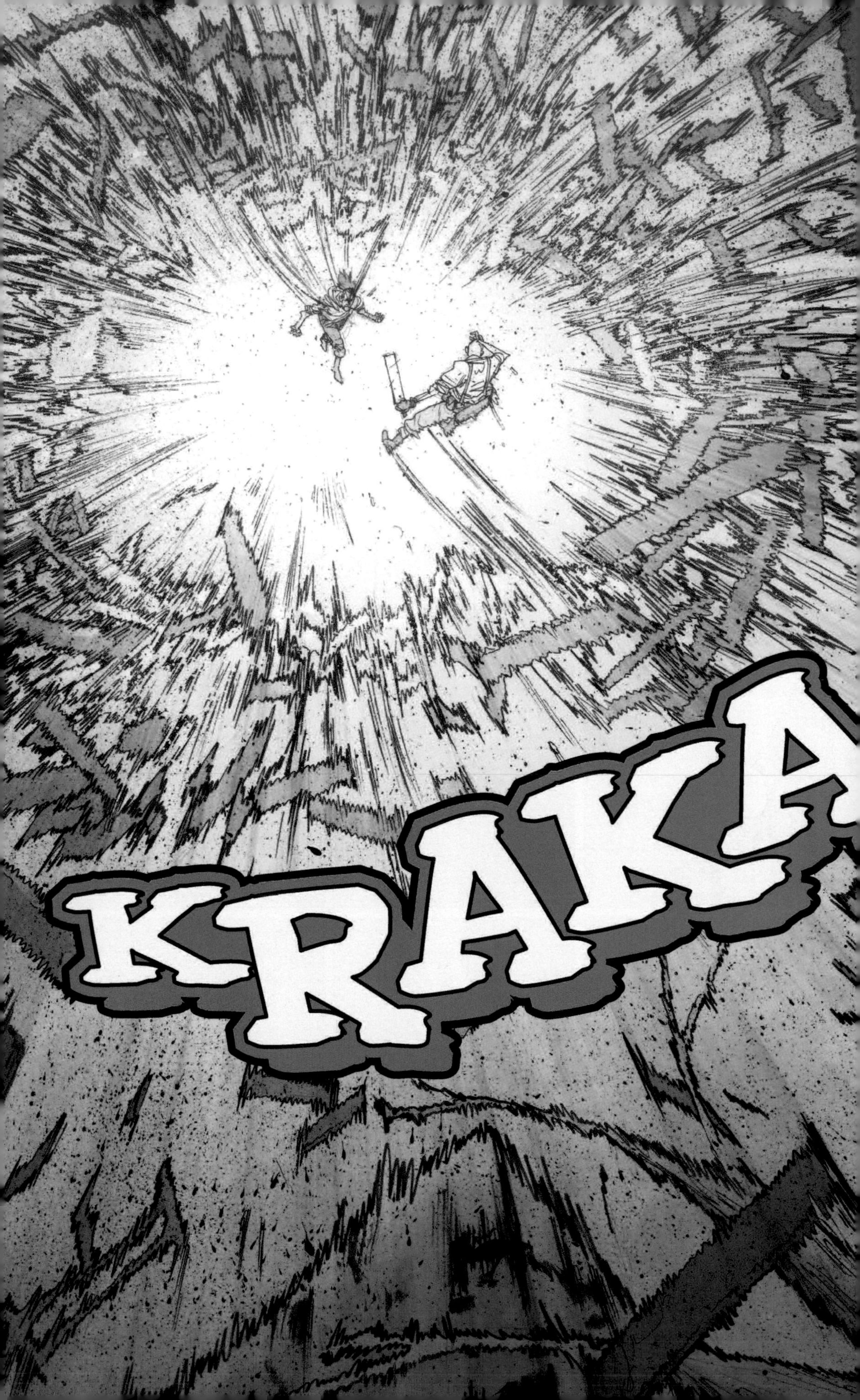
KRAKA

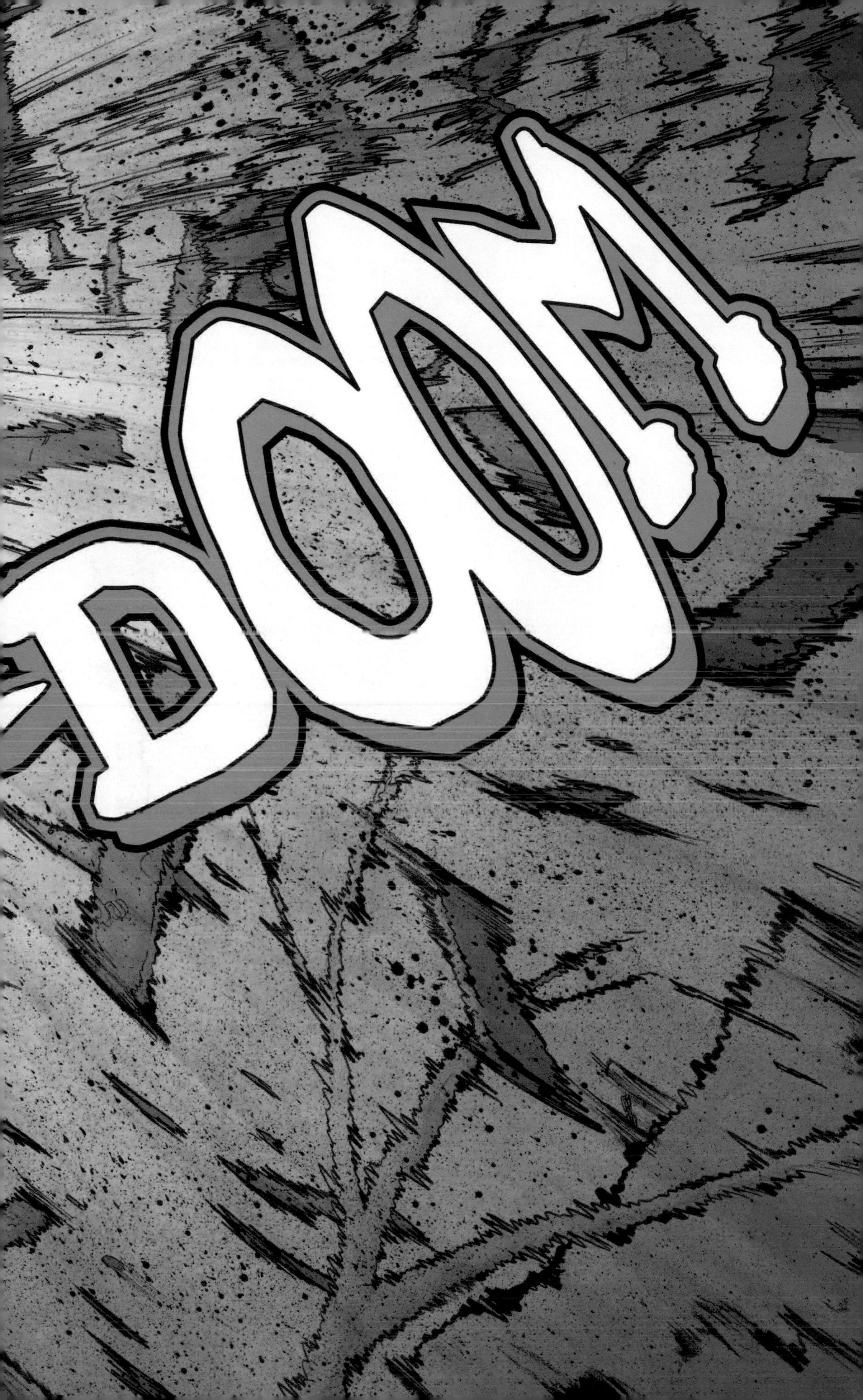
DOOM!

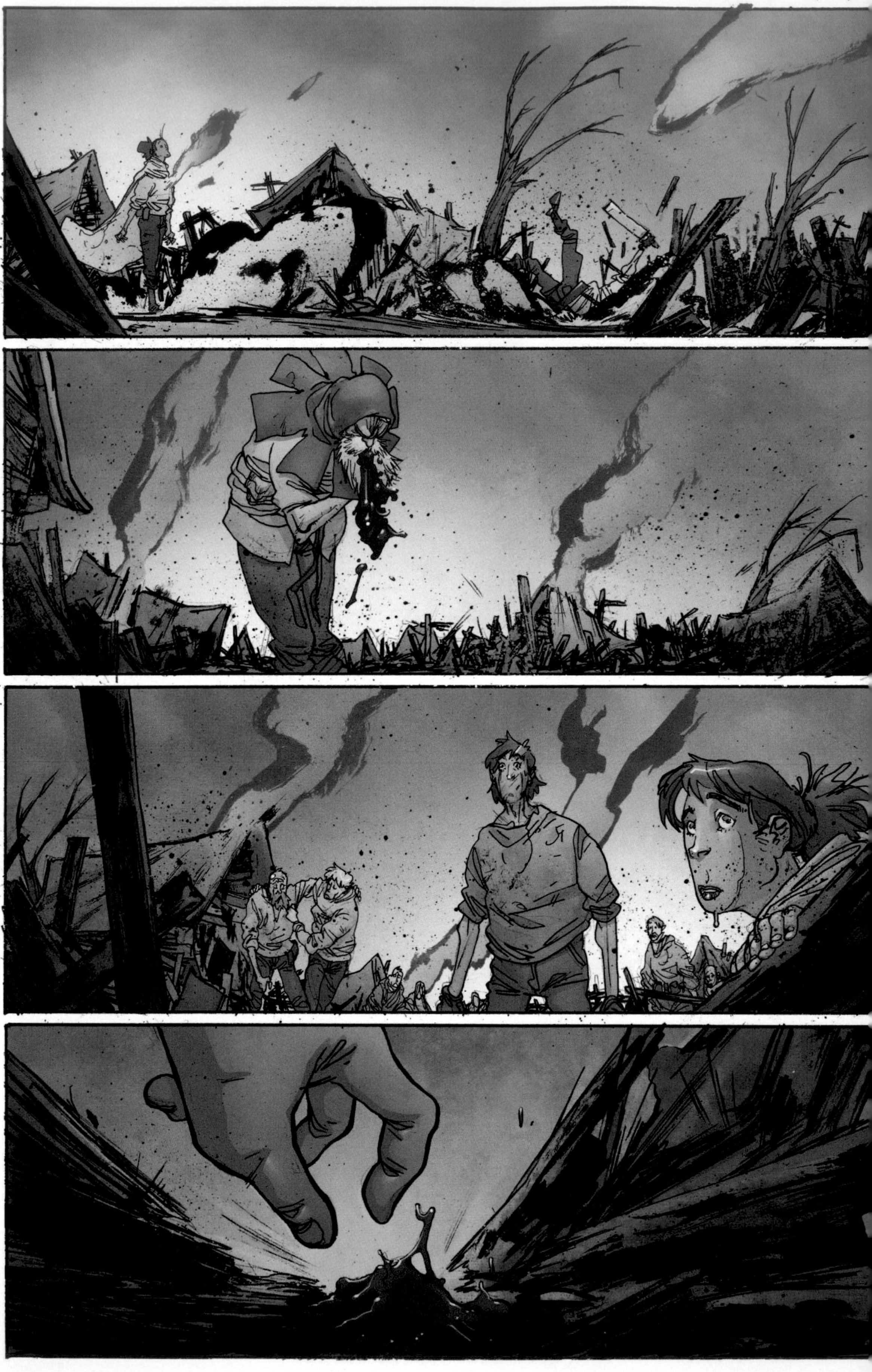

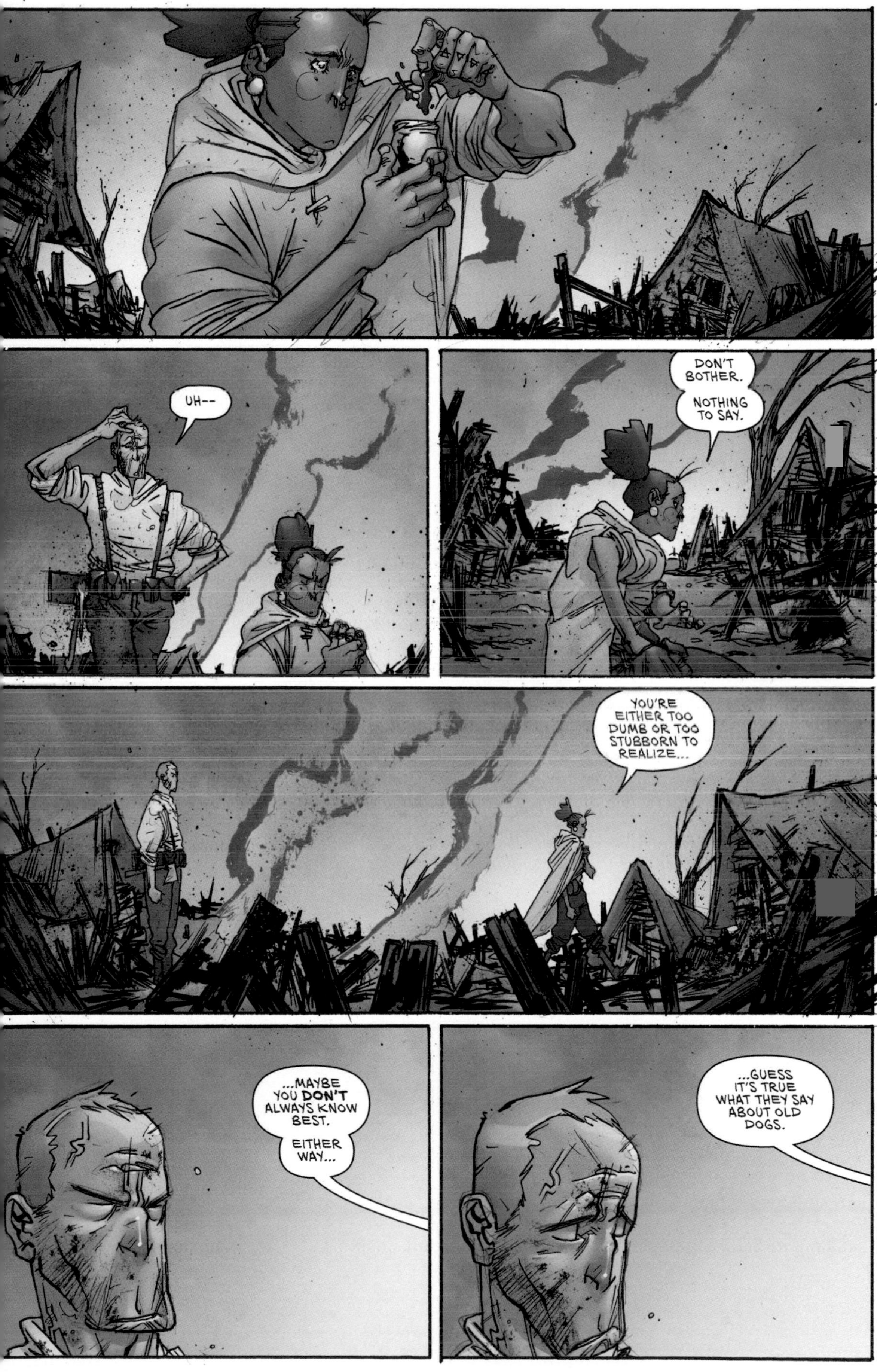
UH--
DON'T BOTHER.
NOTHING TO SAY.
YOU'RE EITHER TOO DUMB OR TOO STUBBORN TO REALIZE...
...MAYBE YOU DON'T ALWAYS KNOW BEST.
EITHER WAY...
...GUESS IT'S TRUE WHAT THEY SAY ABOUT OLD DOGS.

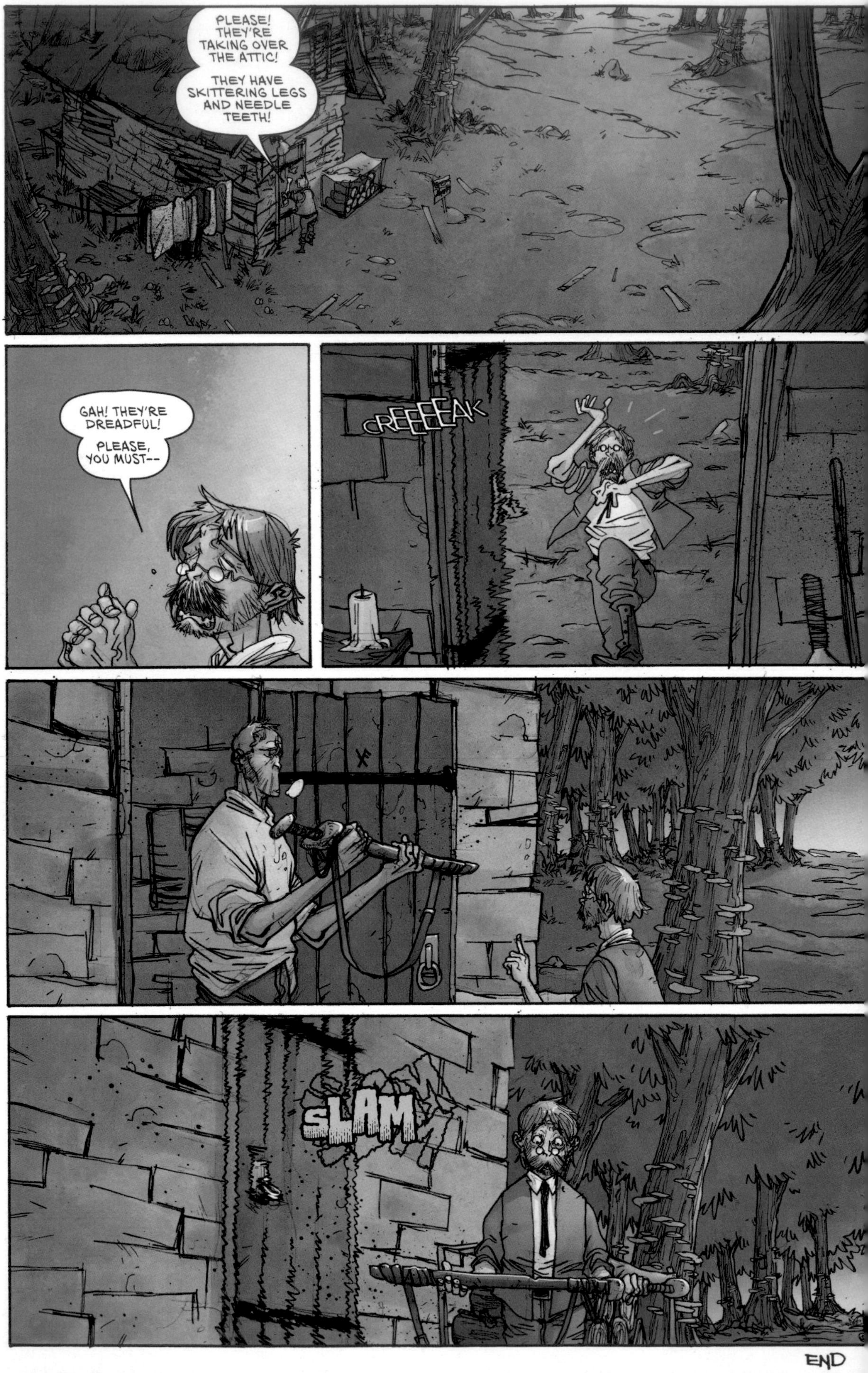
PLEASE! THEY'RE TAKING OVER THE ATTIC!
THEY HAVE SKITTERING LEGS AND NEEDLE TEETH!
GAH! THEY'RE DREADFUL!
PLEASE, YOU MUST--
CREEEEEAK
SLAM
END

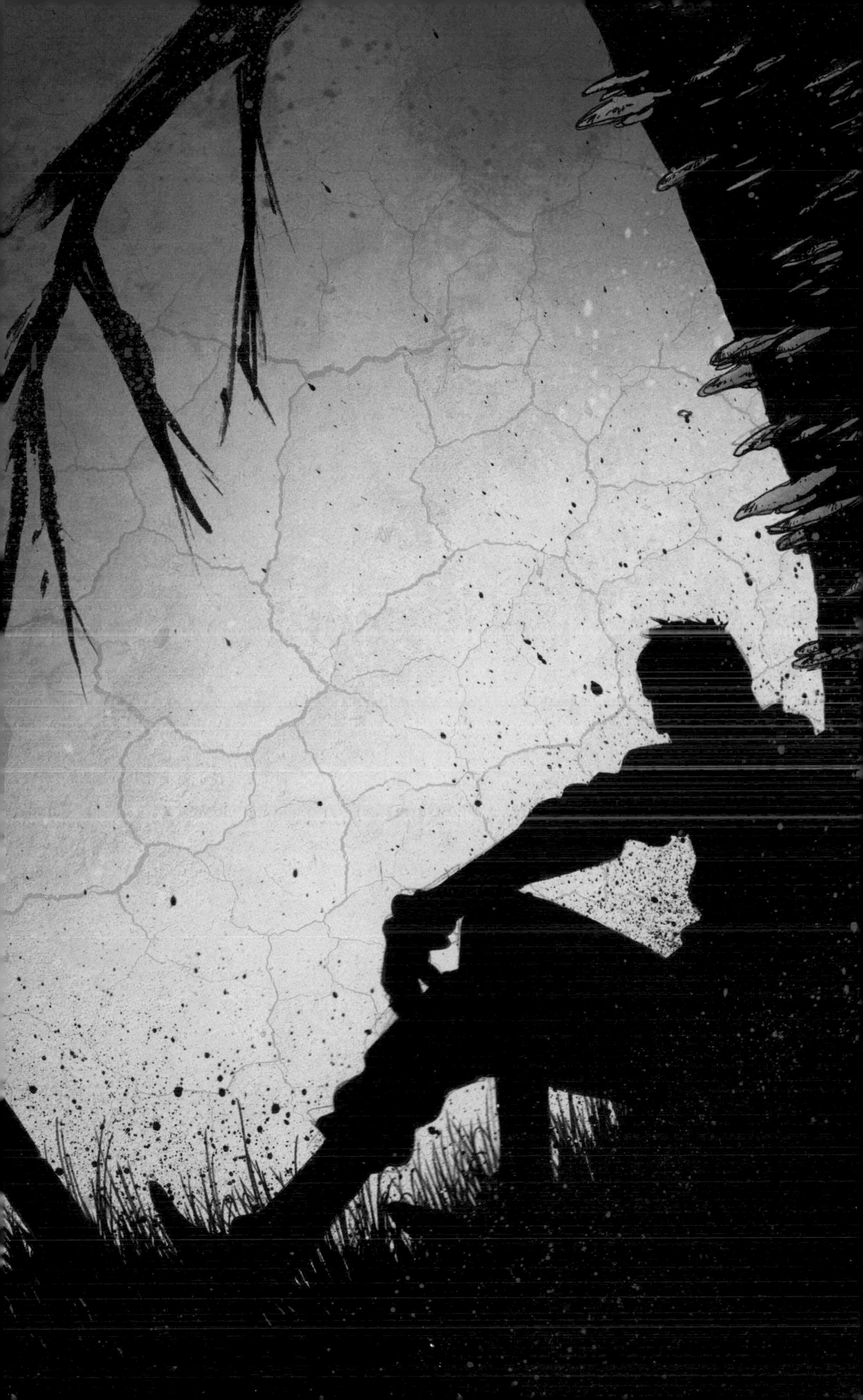

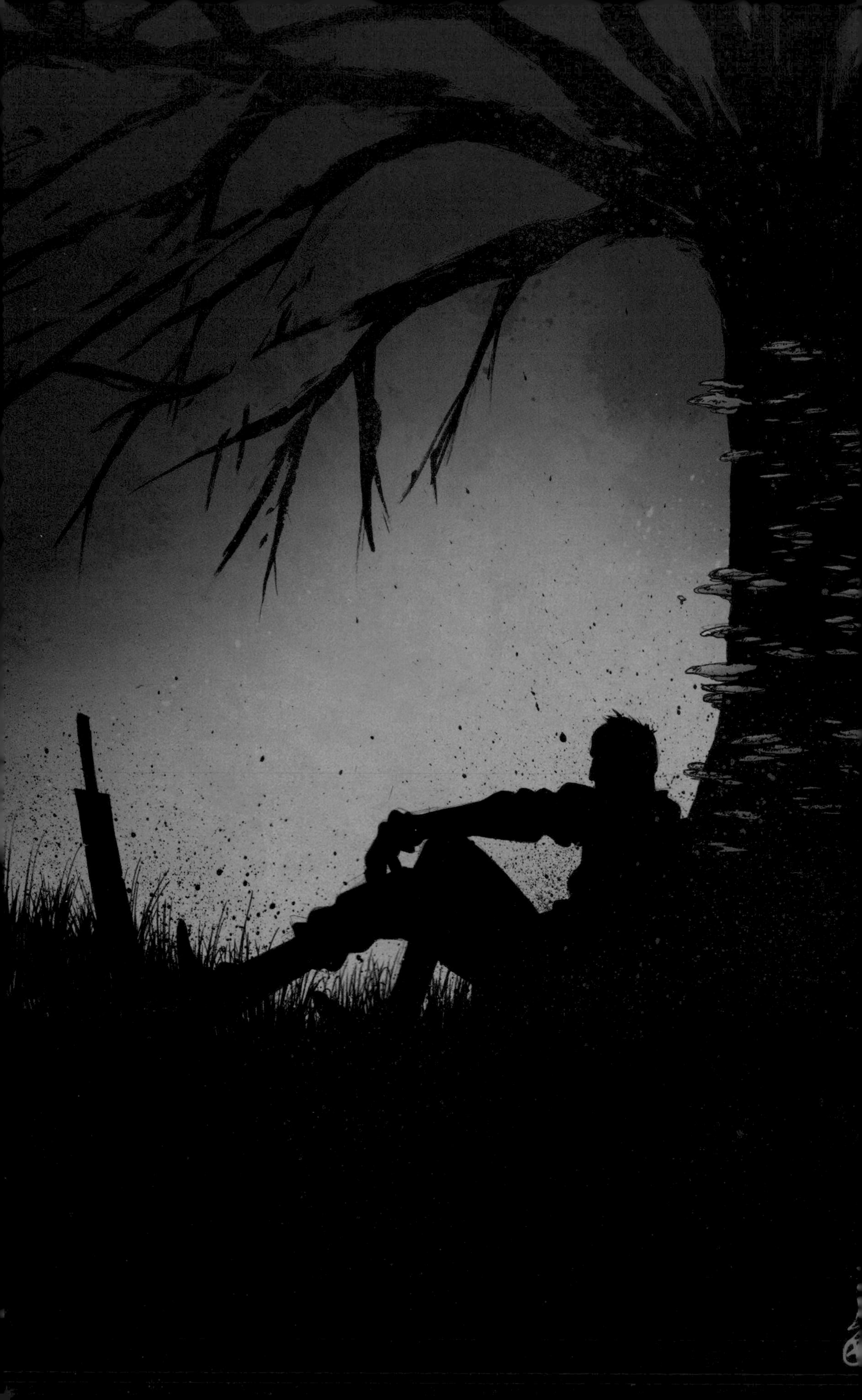

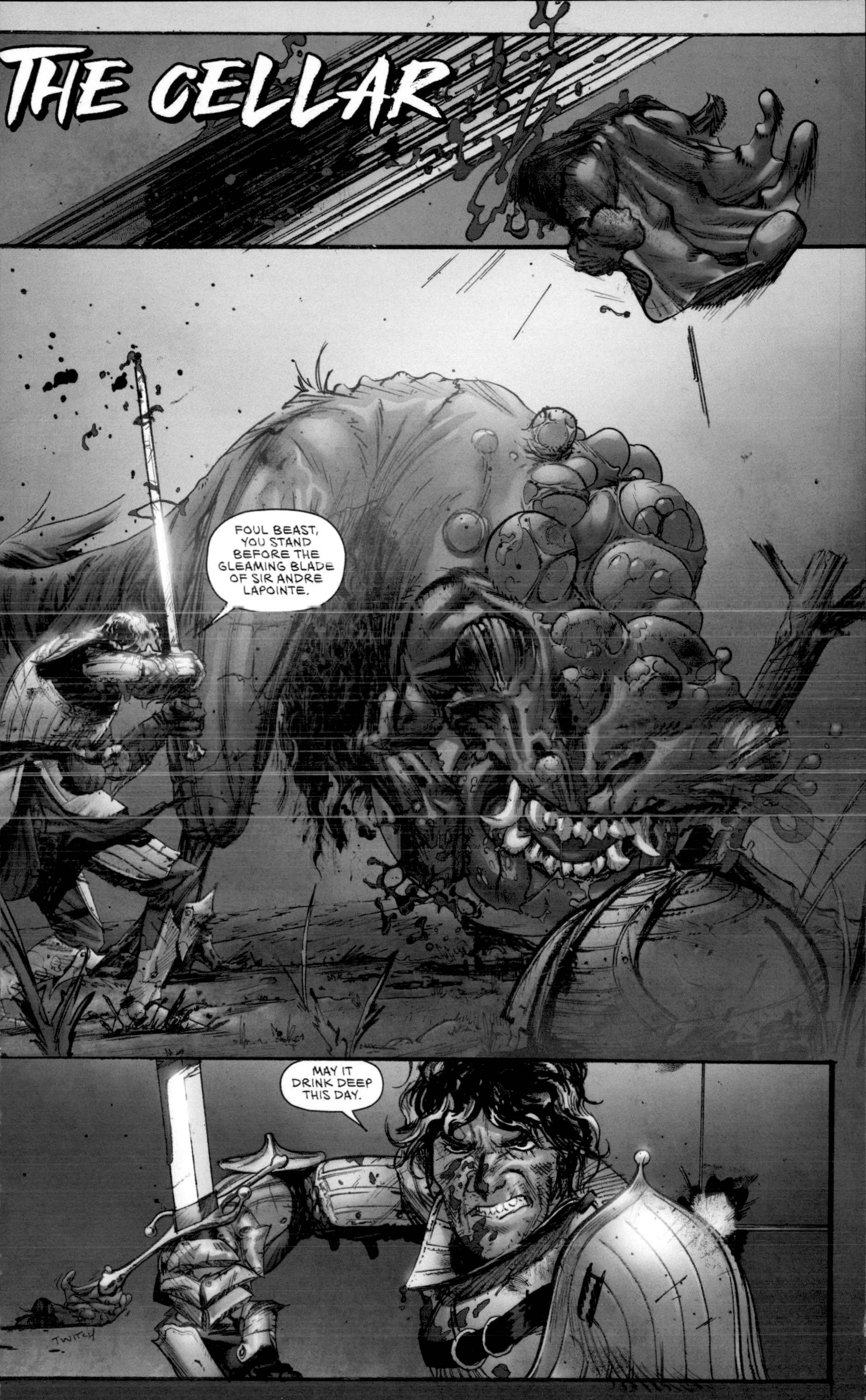
THE CELLAR
FOUL BEAST, YOU STAND BEFORE THE GLEAMING BLADE OF SIR ANDRE LAPOINTE.
MAY IT DRINK DEEP THIS DAY.
TWITCH

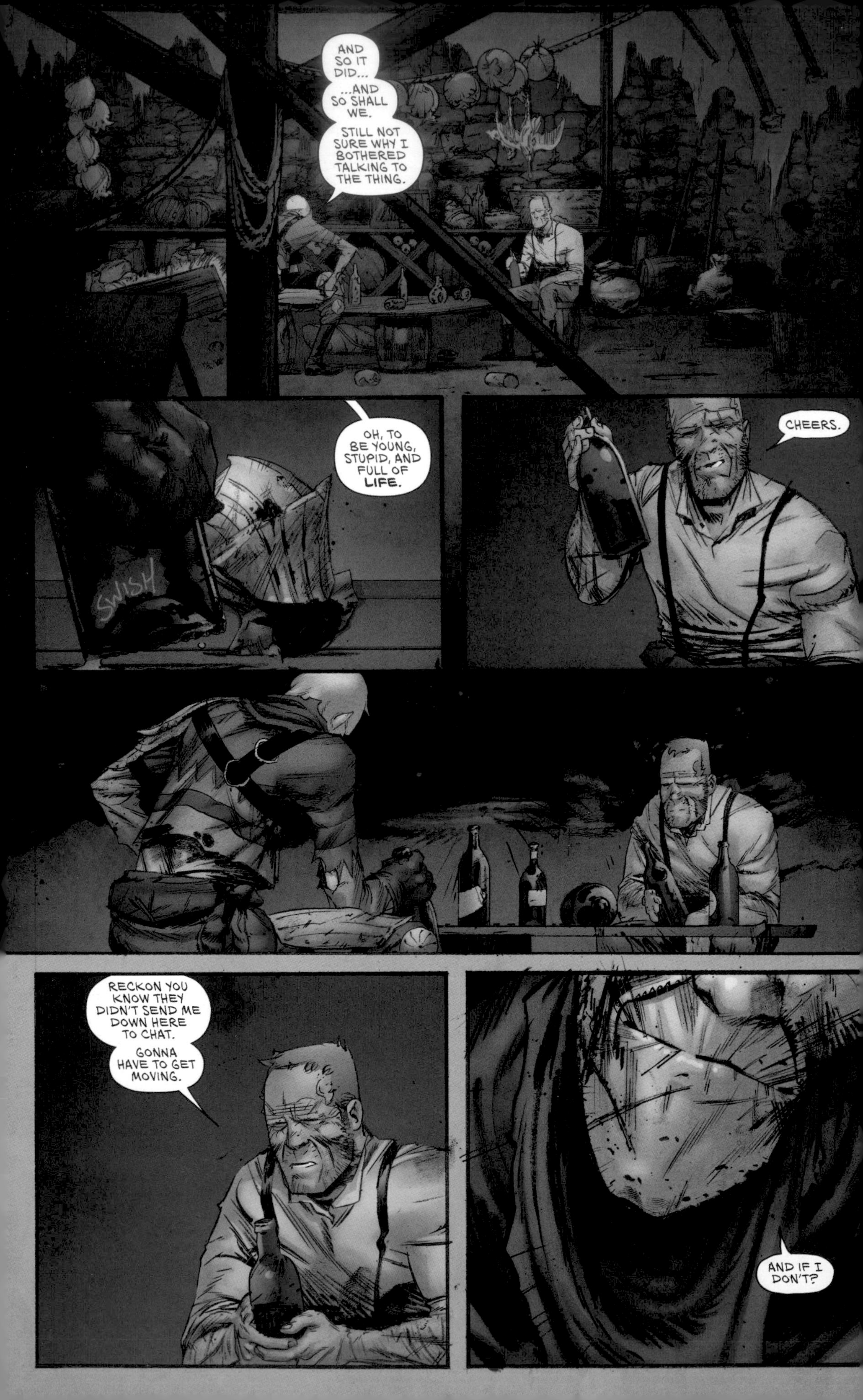
AND SO IT DID...
...AND SO SHALL WE.
STILL NOT SURE WHY I BOTHERED TALKING TO THE THING.
OH, TO BE YOUNG, STUPID, AND FULL OF **LIFE**.
SWISH
CHEERS.
RECKON YOU KNOW THEY DIDN'T SEND ME DOWN HERE TO CHAT.
GONNA HAVE TO GET MOVING.
AND IF I DON'T?

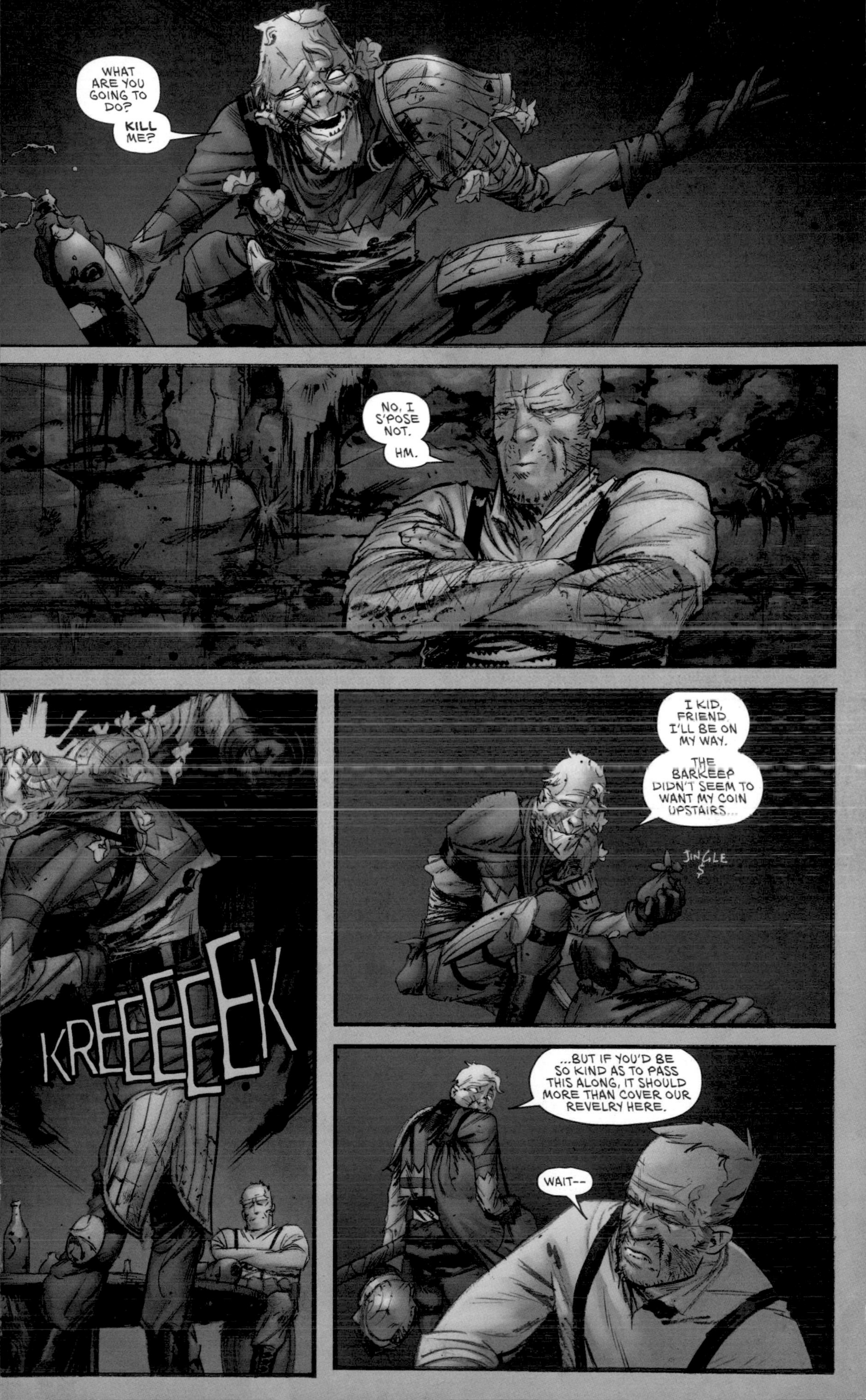
WHAT ARE YOU GOING TO DO?
KILL ME?
NO, I S'POSE NOT.
HM.
KREEEEEEK
I KID, FRIEND. I'LL BE ON MY WAY.
THE BARKEEP DIDN'T SEEM TO WANT MY COIN UPSTAIRS...
JINGLES
...BUT IF YOU'D BE SO KIND AS TO PASS THIS ALONG, IT SHOULD MORE THAN COVER OUR REVELRY HERE.
WAIT--

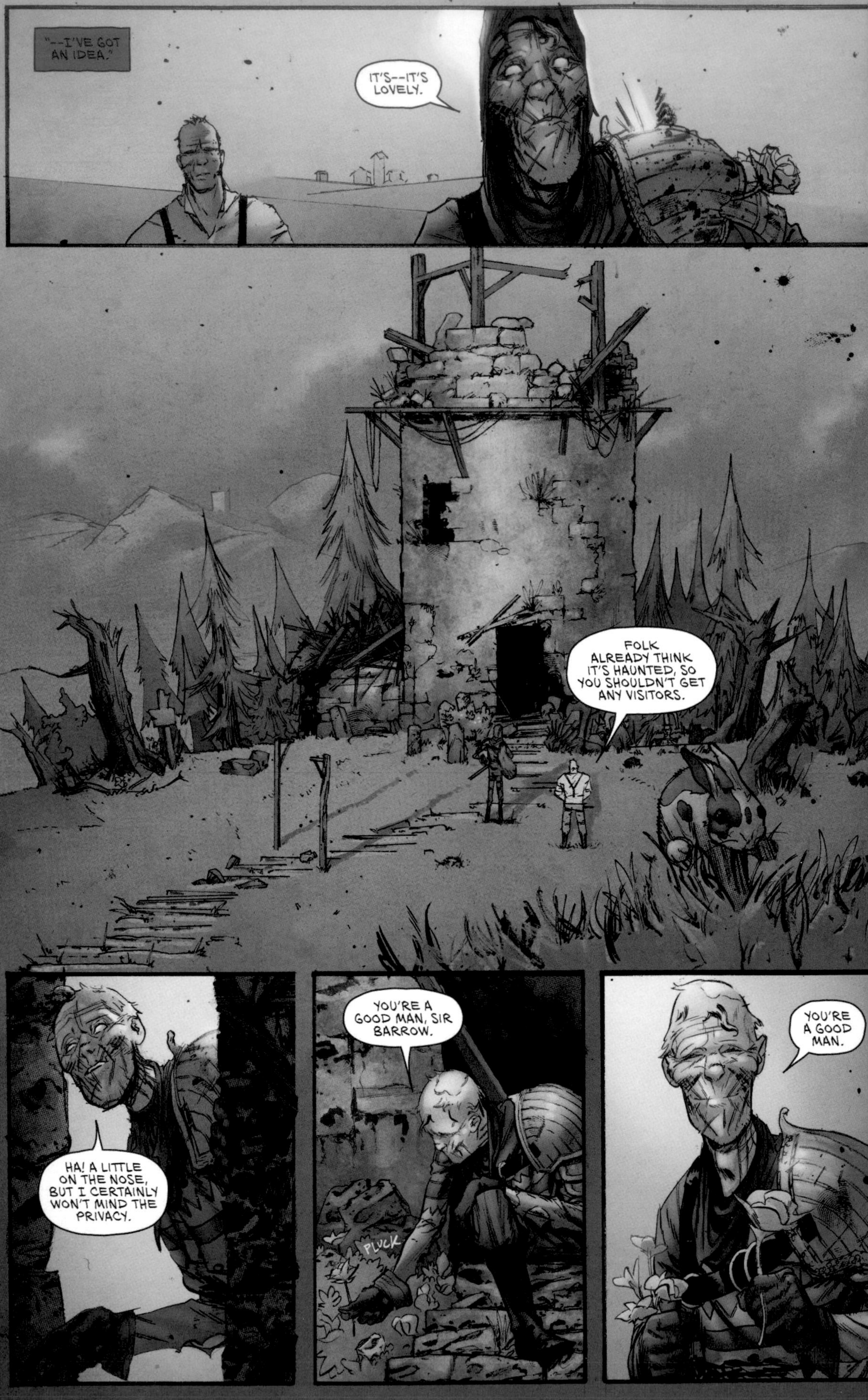
"--I'VE GOT AN IDEA."
IT'S--IT'S LOVELY.
FOLK ALREADY THINK IT'S HAUNTED, SO YOU SHOULDN'T GET ANY VISITORS.
HA! A LITTLE ON THE NOSE, BUT I CERTAINLY WON'T MIND THE PRIVACY.
YOU'RE A GOOD MAN, SIR BARROW.
PLUCK
YOU'RE A GOOD MAN.

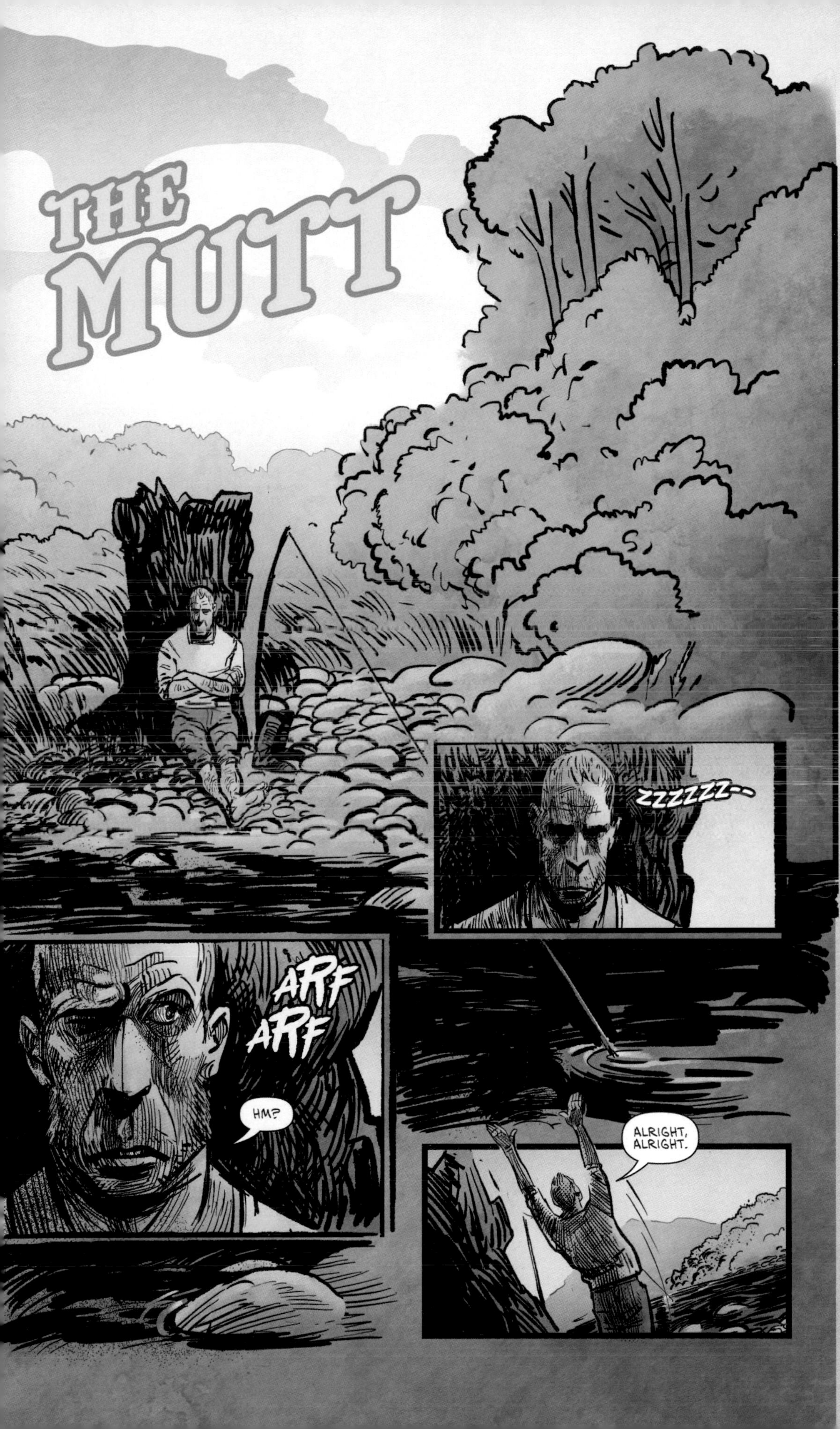
THE MUTT
ZZZZZZ--
ARF
ARF
HM?
ALRIGHT, ALRIGHT.

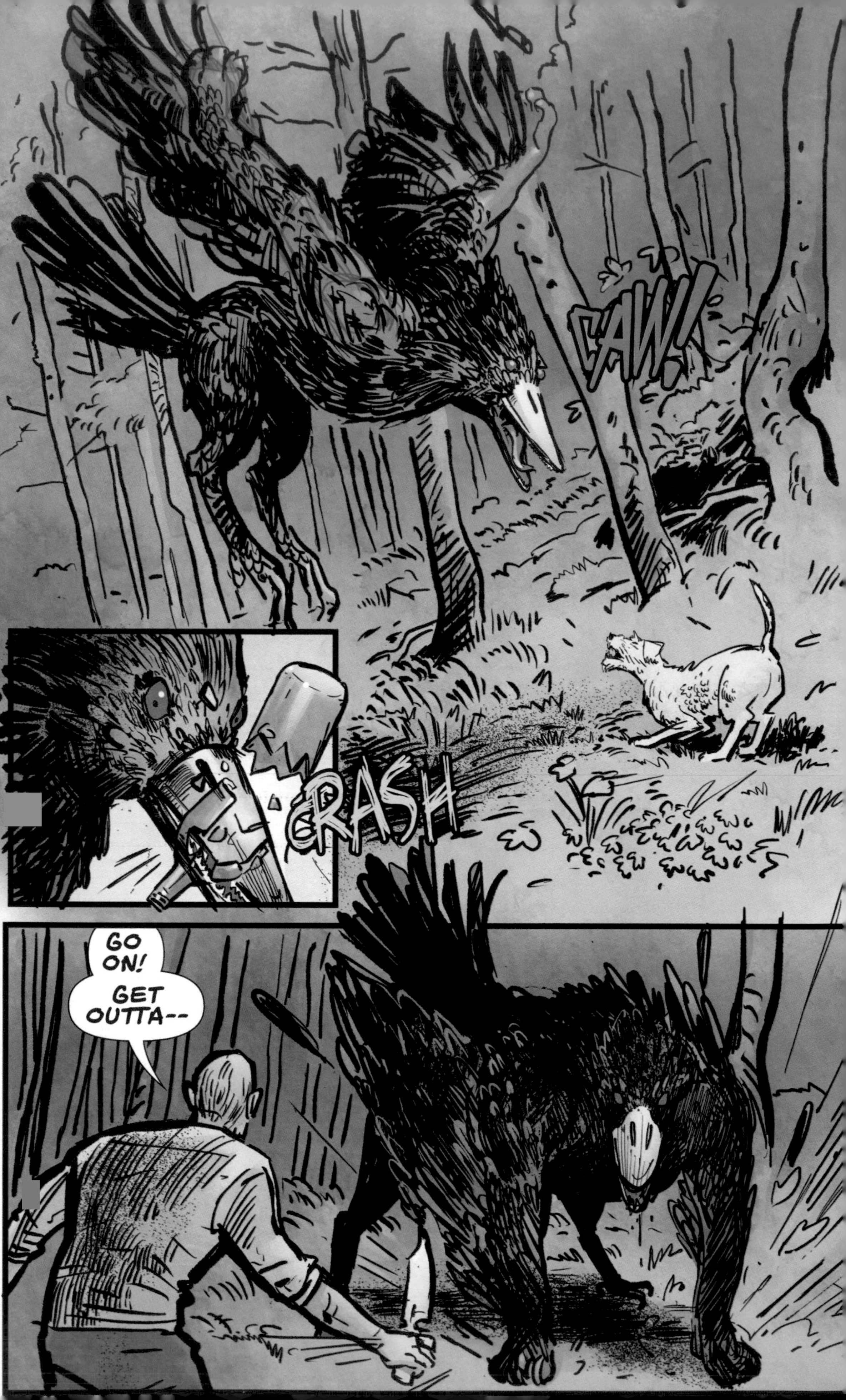
CAW!!
CRASH
GO ON! GET OUTTA--

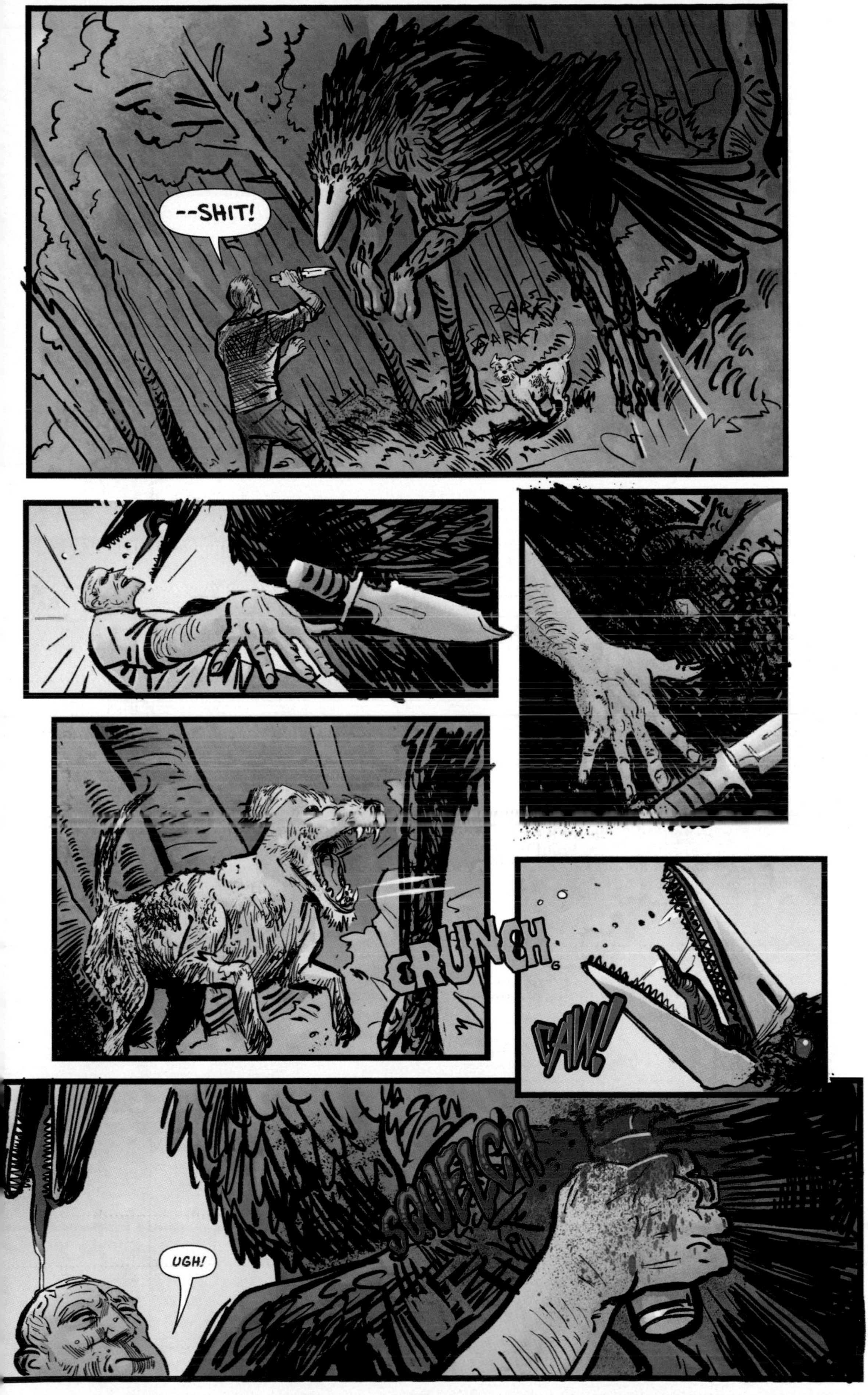
--SHIT!
BARK! BARK!
CRUNCH
CAW!
SQUELCH
UGH!

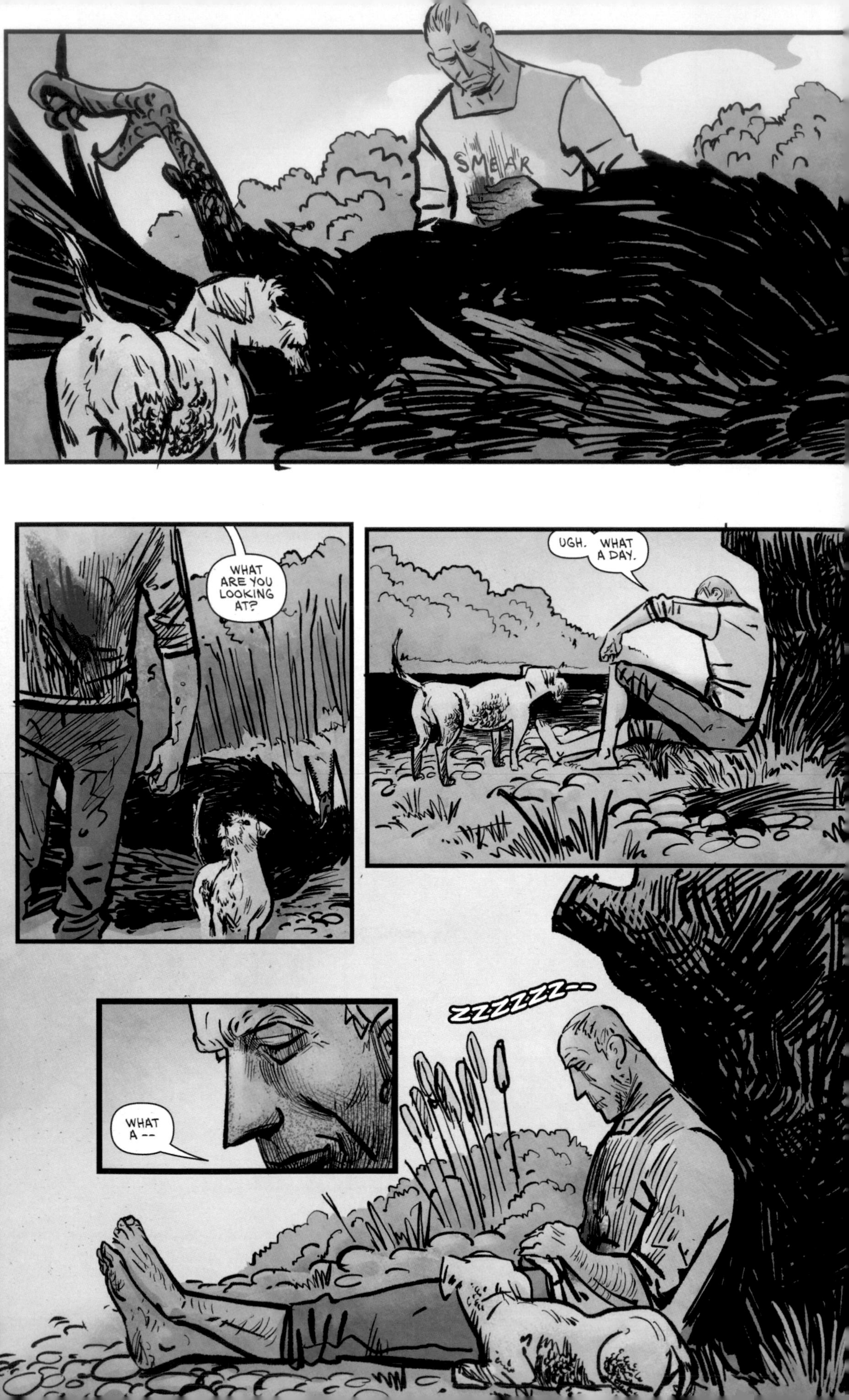
SMEAR
WHAT ARE YOU LOOKING AT?
UGH. WHAT A DAY.
WHAT A --
ZZZZZZ--

GRIT
CREATIVE TEAM

BRIAN WICKMAN is a comic writer and public librarian living in Baltimore, Maryland. He is the co-creator of the comics GRIT and BIG WHITE.

KEVIN CASTANIERO is a freelance illustrator hailing from sunny California, where he spends most of his time drawing intestines and petting his two cats.

SIMON GOUGH is a comic book colourist from the UK, hailing from Birmingham, in the Midlands. He has worked on properties such as G.I Joe, TMNT, Ringside, and the Aliens/Predator franchises.

MICAH MYERS is a comic book letterer from Portsmouth, Virginia. He has lettered comics for Image, Dark Horse, IDW, Scout, Starburns, Heavy Metal, Mad Cave, Devil's Due, and many more.

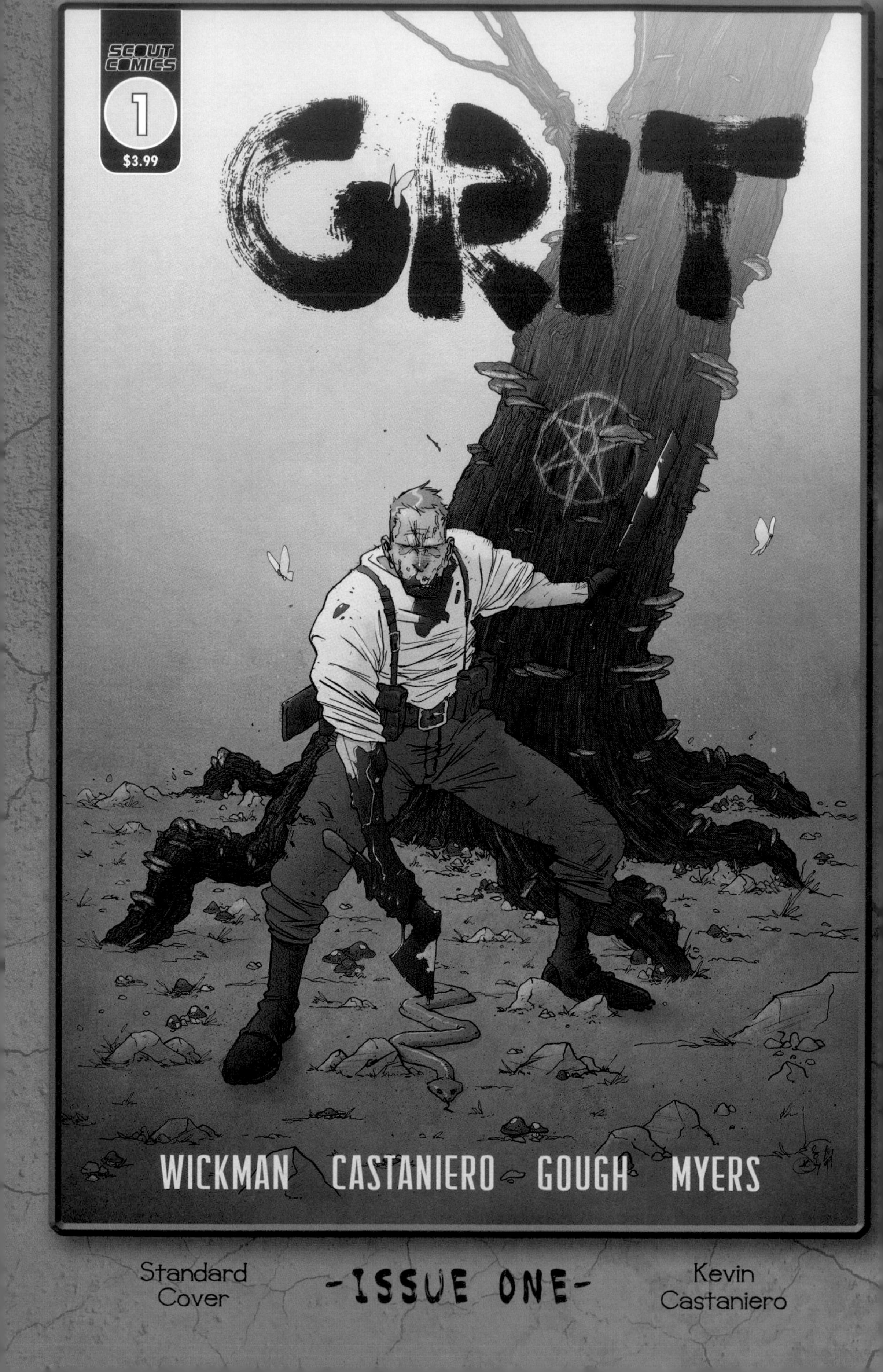
SCOUT COMICS
1
$3.99
GRIT
WICKMAN CASTANIERO GOUGH MYERS

Standard Cover

-ISSUE ONE-

Kevin Castaniero

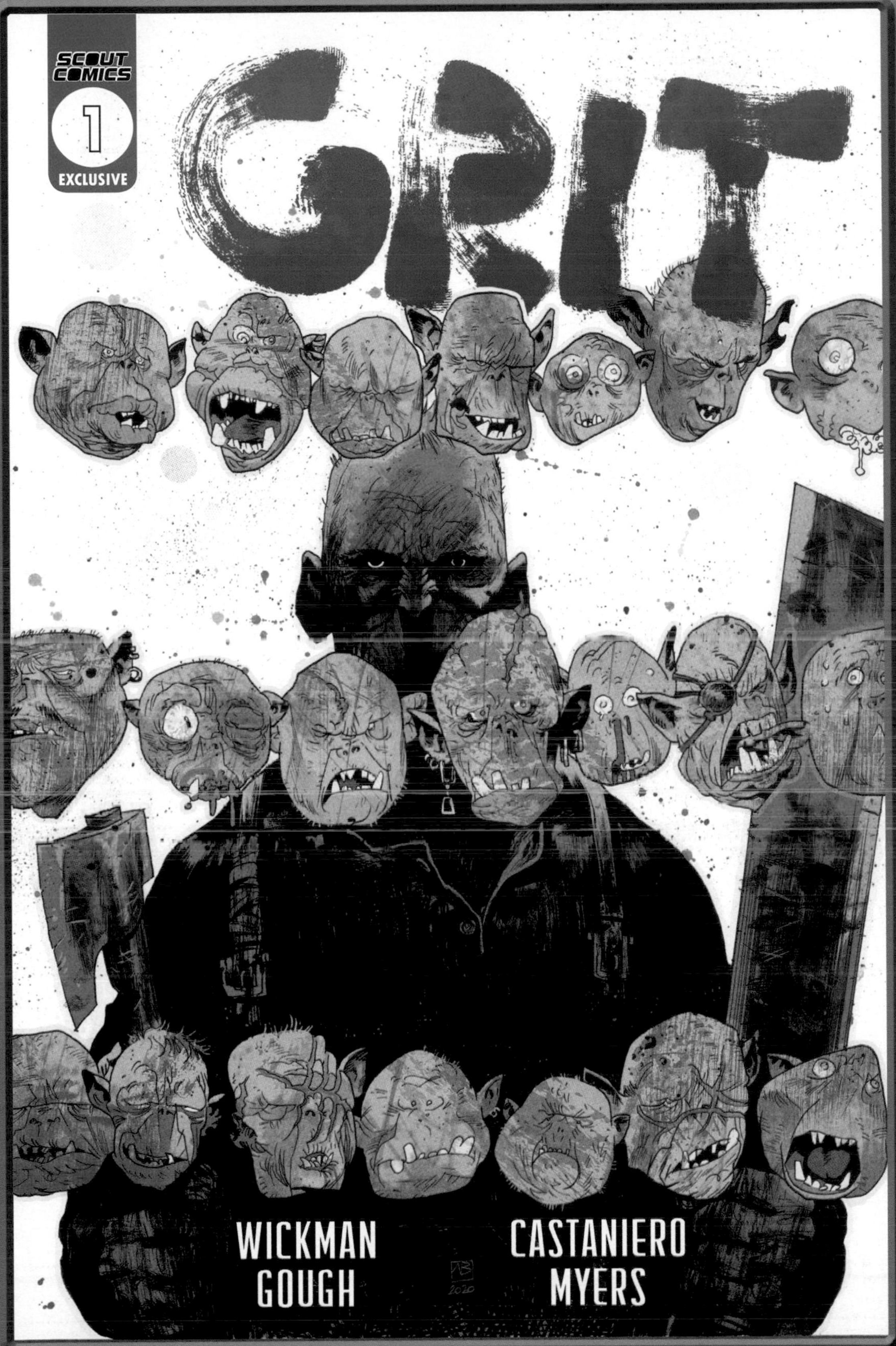
SCOUT COMICS
1
EXCLUSIVE
GRIT
WICKMAN
GOUGH
CASTANIERO
MYERS
2020

Space Cadets Exclusive

-ISSUE ONE-

Kevin Castaniero

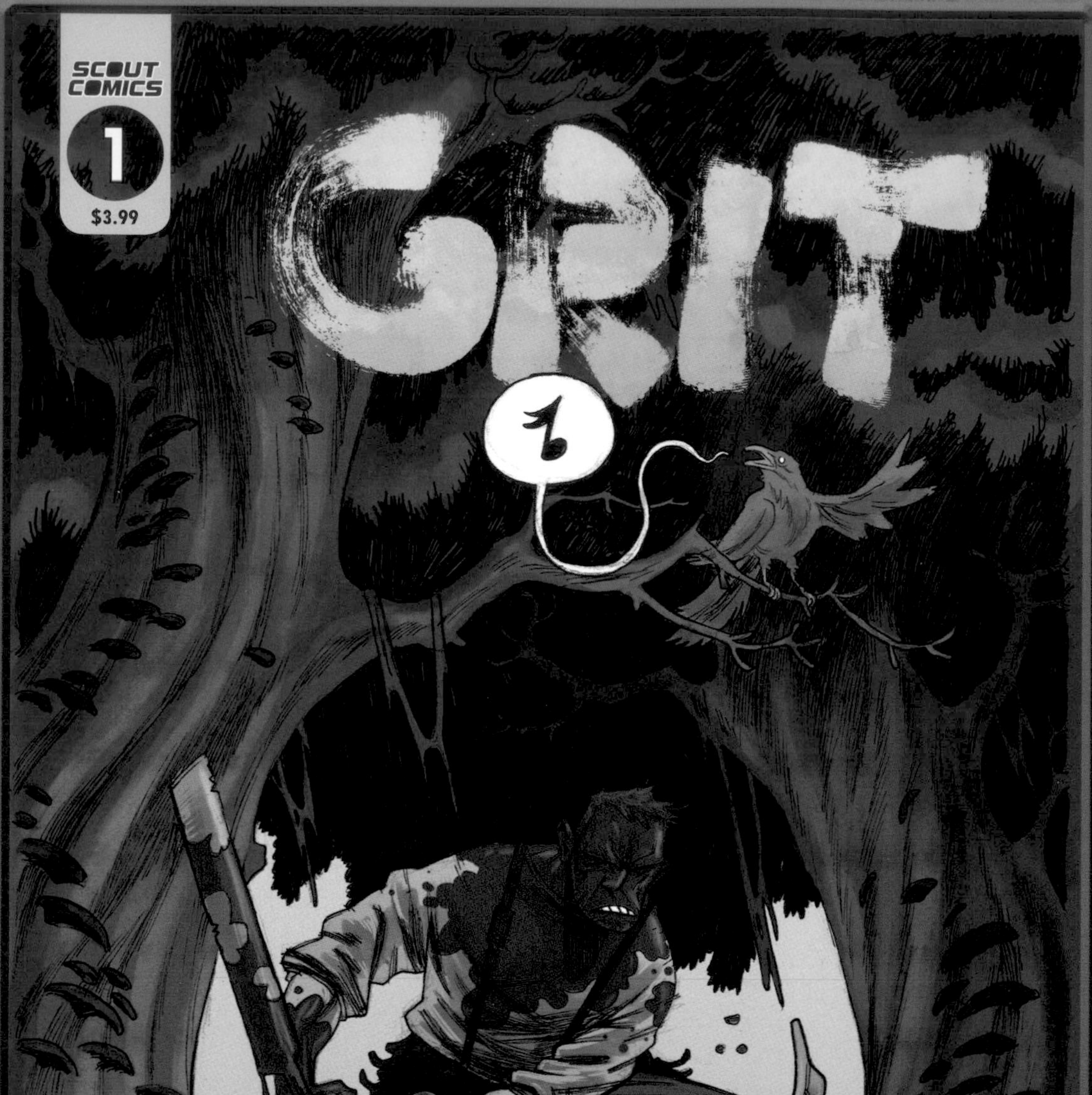

Second Printing

-ISSUE ONE-

Mark Laszlo

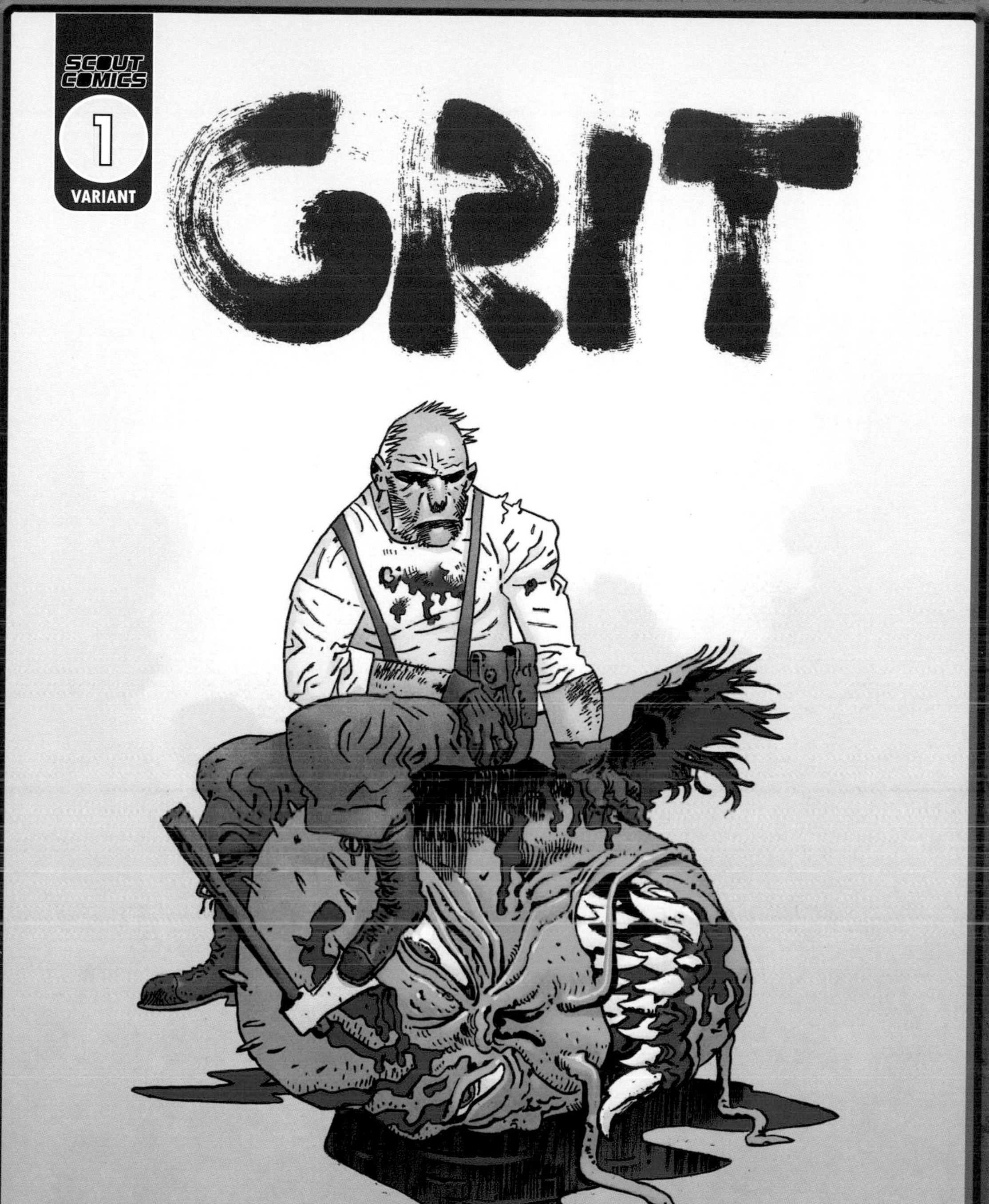
SCOUT COMICS
1
VARIANT
GRIT
WICKMAN CASTANIERO GOUGH MYERS

Scout Webstore — -ISSUE ONE- — Artyom Trakhanov

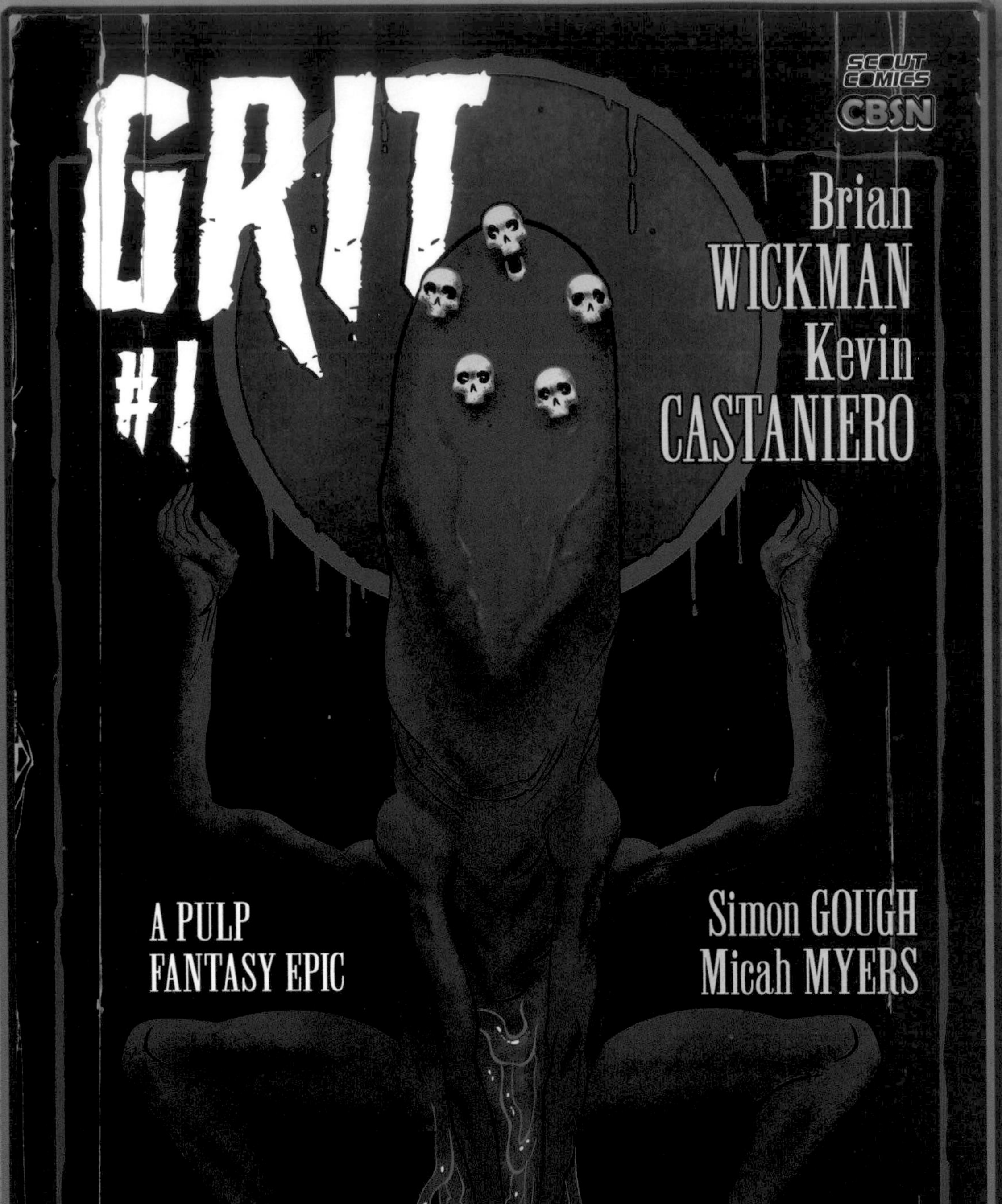

CBSN Variant

-ISSUE ONE-

Goran Gligović

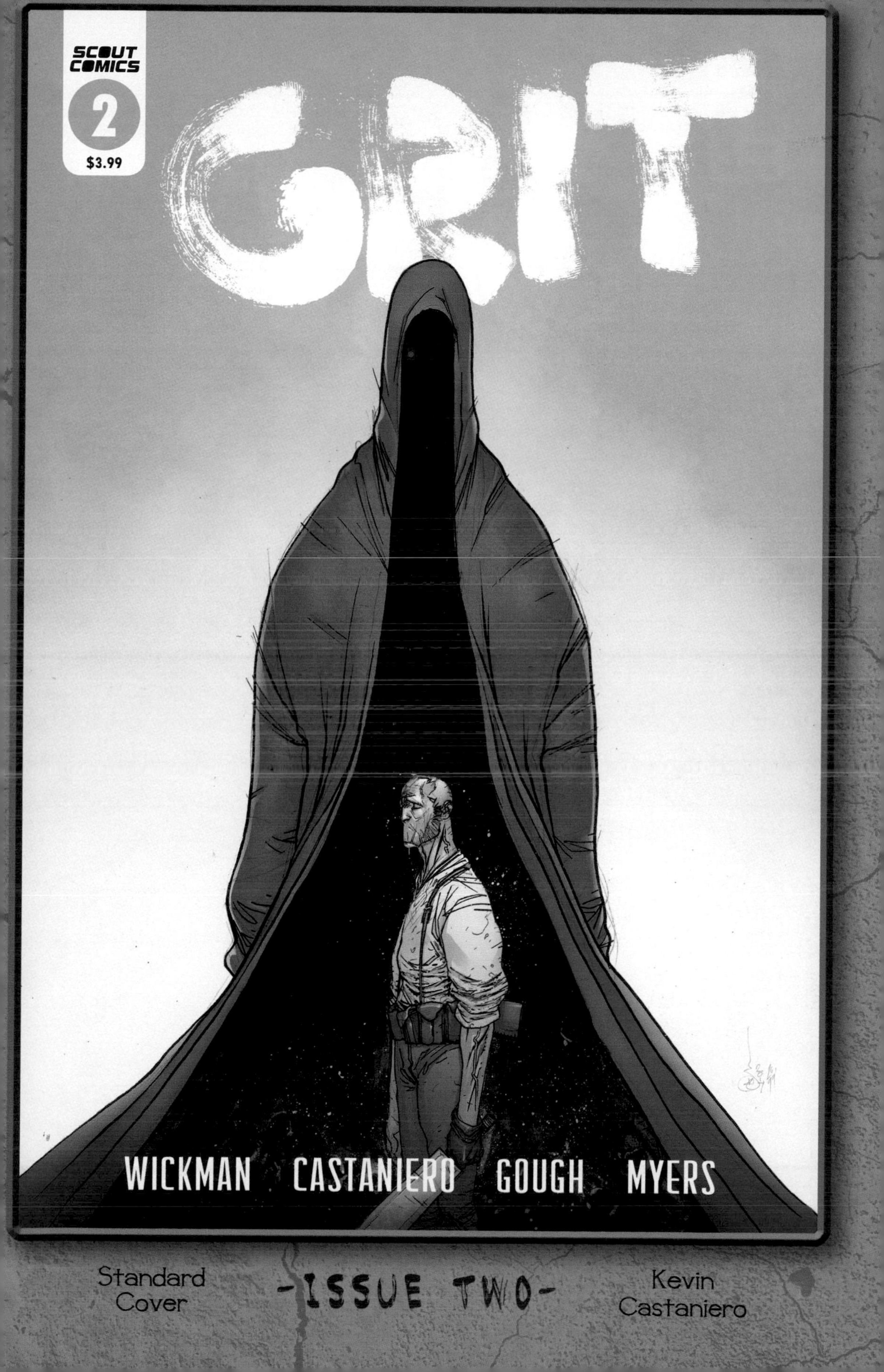
SCOUT COMICS
2
$3.99
GRIT
WICKMAN CASTANIERO GOUGH MYERS

Standard Cover

-ISSUE TWO-

Kevin Castaniero

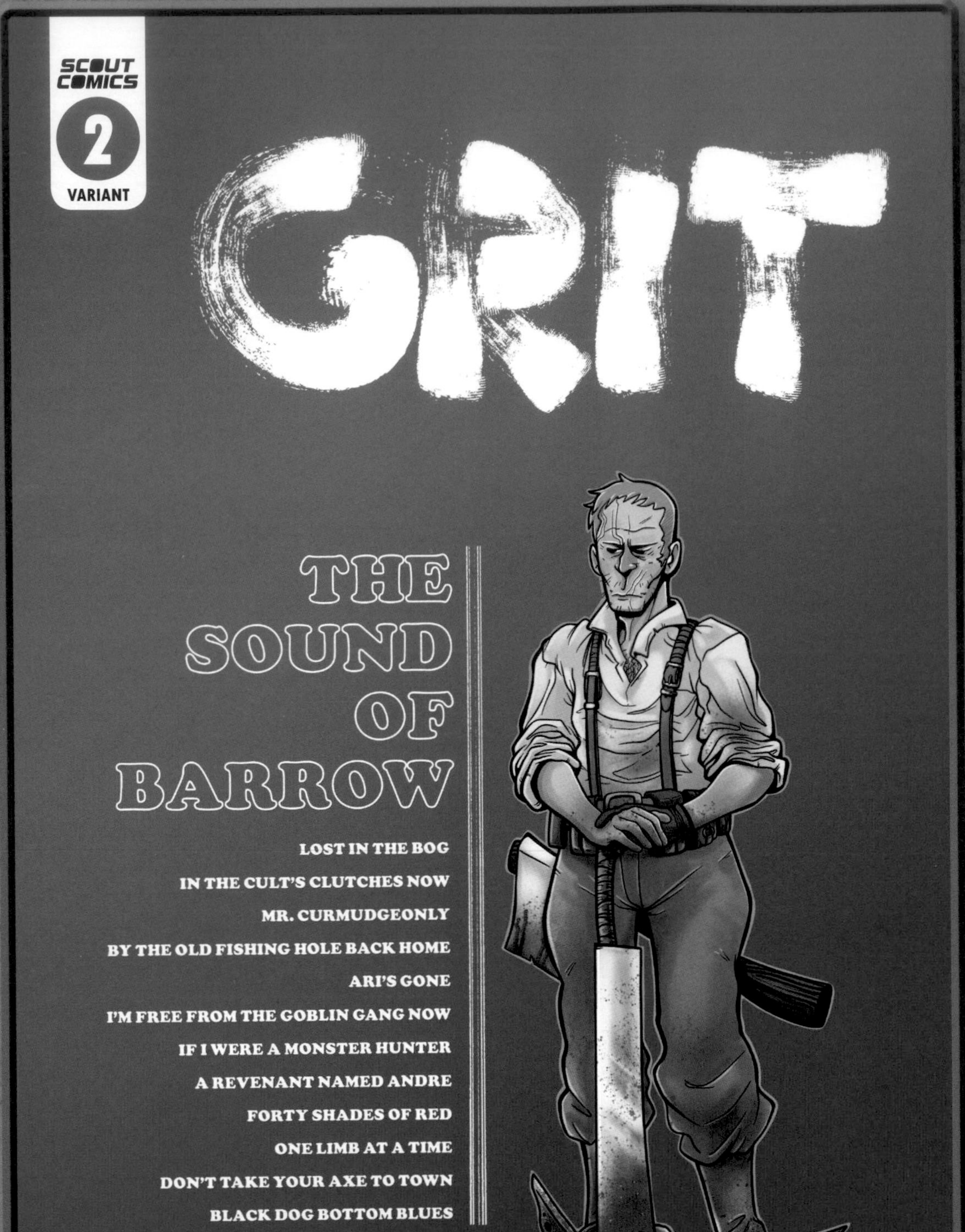
SCOUT COMICS
2
VARIANT
GRIT
THE SOUND OF BARROW
LOST IN THE BOG
IN THE CULT'S CLUTCHES NOW
MR. CURMUDGEONLY
BY THE OLD FISHING HOLE BACK HOME
ARI'S GONE
I'M FREE FROM THE GOBLIN GANG NOW
IF I WERE A MONSTER HUNTER
A REVENANT NAMED ANDRE
FORTY SHADES OF RED
ONE LIMB AT A TIME
DON'T TAKE YOUR AXE TO TOWN
BLACK DOG BOTTOM BLUES
WICKMAN CASTANIERO GOUGH MYERS

Scout Webstore -ISSUE TWO- Ally Cat

SCOUT
COMICS

2

$3.99

GRIT

WICKMAN   CASTANIERO   GOUGH   MYERS

Second
Printing

-ISSUE TWO-

Te'Shawn
Dwyer

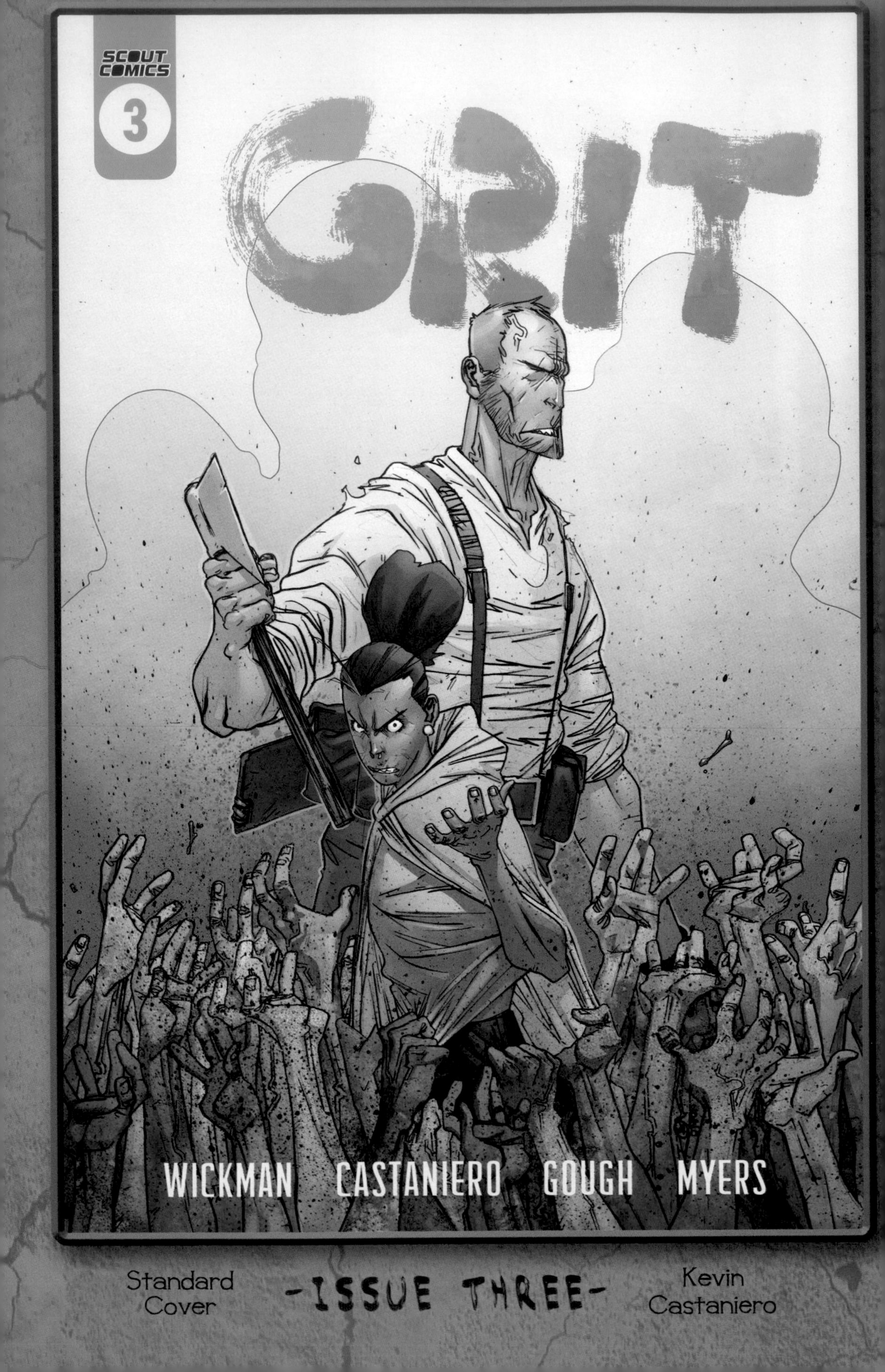
SCOUT COMICS
3
GRIT
WICKMAN CASTANIERO GOUGH MYERS

Standard Cover

-ISSUE THREE-

Kevin Castaniero